PRIMARY MATHEMATICS

TEXTBOOK 4A

Common Core Edition

SINGAPORE
MATH®
PROGRAM

Marshall Cavendish
Education

US Distributor

SM Singapore Math Inc.®

BLANK

Original edition published under the title Primary Mathematics Textbook 4A
© 1981 Curriculum Planning & Development Division, Ministry of Education, Singapore
Published by Times Media Private Limited

This edition © 2014 Marshall Cavendish Education Pte Ltd

Published by Marshall Cavendish Education
Times Centre, 1 New Industrial Road, Singapore 536196
Customer Service Hotline: (65) 6213 9444
US Office Tel: (1-914) 332 8888 | Fax: (1-914) 332 8882
E-mail: tmesales@mceducation.com
Website: www.mceducation.com

Distributed by
Singapore Math Inc.®
19535 SW 129th Avenue
Tualatin, OR 97062, U.S.A.
Tel: (503) 557 8100
Website: www.singaporemath.com

First published 2014
Reprinted 2014, 2015, 2016

Primary Mathematics (Common Core Edition) Textbook 4A
ISBN 978-981-01-9835-0

Printed in Malaysia

Primary Mathematics (Common Core Edition) is adapted from Primary Mathematics Textbook 4A (3rd Edition),
originally developed by the Ministry of Education, Singapore. This edition contains new content developed by
Marshall Cavendish Education Pte Ltd, which is not attributable to the Ministry of Education, Singapore.

We would like to acknowledge the contributions by:

The Project Team from the Ministry of Education, Singapore that developed the original Singapore edition
Project Director: Dr Kho Tek Hong
Team Members: Hector Chee Kum Hoong, Liang Hin Hoon, Lim Eng Tann, Ng Siew Lee, Rosalind Lim Hui Cheng,
Ng Hwee Wan

Primary Mathematics (Common Core Edition)
Richard Askey, Emeritus Professor of Mathematics from University of Wisconsin, Madison
Jennifer Kempe, Curriculum Advisor from Singapore Math Inc.®

PRIMARY MATHEMATICS Common Core Edition is a complete program from Marshall Cavendish Education the publishers of Singapore's successful *Primary Mathematics* series. Newly adapted to align with the Common Core State Standards for mathematics, the program aims to equip students with sound concept development, critical thinking and efficient problem-solving skills.

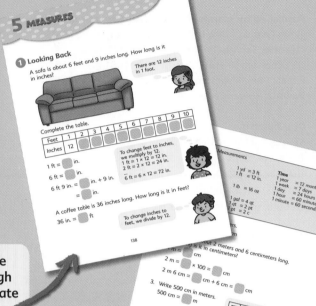

Mathematical concepts are introduced in the opening pages and taught to mastery through specific learning tasks that allow for immediate assessment and consolidation.

The **modeling method** enables students to visualize and solve mathematical problems quickly and efficiently.

The Concrete → Pictorial → Abstract approach enables students to encounter math in a meaningful way and translate mathematical skills from the concrete to the abstract.

The **pencil icon** ✏️ Exercise 3, pages 44–45 provides quick and easy reference from the Textbook to the relevant Workbook pages. The **direct correlation** of the Workbook to the Textbook facilitates focused review and evaluation.

New mathematical concepts are introduced through a **spiral progression** that builds on concepts already taught and mastered.

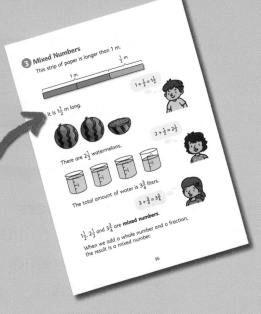

3 Mixed Numbers

This strip of paper is longer than 1 m.

It is $1\frac{1}{2}$ m long.

$1 + \frac{1}{2} = 1\frac{1}{2}$

There are $2\frac{1}{2}$ watermelons.

$2 + \frac{1}{2} = 2\frac{1}{2}$

The total amount of water is $3\frac{3}{4}$ liters.

$3 + \frac{3}{4} = 3\frac{3}{4}$

$1\frac{1}{2}$, $2\frac{1}{2}$ and $3\frac{3}{4}$ are **mixed numbers**.

When we add a whole number and a fraction, the result is a mixed number.

95

To round a number to the nearest ten thousand, we can look at the digit in the thousands place. If it is 5 or greater than 5, we round up. If it is smaller than 5, we round down.

7. Round each number to the nearest ten thousand.
   (a) 49,287 ≈ 50,000
   (b) 73,501 ≈
   (c) 804,390 ≈
   (d) 129,500 ≈

8. Round 836,529 to the nearest hundred thousand.

The digit 8 is in the hundred thousands place.
836,529
What digit is in the next lower place?
836,529
Do we round up or down?

836,529 ≈ when it is rounded to the nearest hundred thousand.

We round up. 796,030 rounded to the nearest hundred thousand is 800,000.

9. What is 796,030 to the nearest hundred thousand?

10. Round each number to the nearest thousand, ten thousand, and hundred thousand.
    (a) 243,700
    (b) 138,465
    (c)
    (d) 349,999
    (e) 99,501
    () 567,501
    () 651,491

Exercise 6, pages 19–20

23

Metacognition is employed as a strategy for learners to monitor their thinking processes in problem solving. Speech and thought bubbles provide guidance through the thought processes, making even the most challenging problems accessible to students.

The **color patch** [ ] is used to invite active student participation and to facilitate lively discussion about the mathematical concepts taught.

REVIEW 5

1. Morris made 8 L 75 ml of fruit punch. How much fruit punch did he make in milliliters?
   (A) 8,750 ml   (B) 8,075 ml
   (C) 875 ml   (D) 87,500 ml

2. Ruth ran 2 km 950 m last week. Tricia ran 3 times as far. How much further did Tricia run than Ruth?
   (A) 5 km 900 m   (B) 5 km 950 m
   (C) 6 km 950 m   (D) 8 km 850 m

3. What fraction of 1 gal is 4 c?
   (A) $\frac{4}{1}$ (B) $\frac{1}{2}$ (C) $\frac{1}{4}$ (D) $\frac{1}{8}$

4. Select True or False for the following.
   (a) 3 h 15 min × 4 < 13 h   True / False
   (b) 6 m 20 cm ÷ 5 = 1 m 4 cm   True / False

5. Select True or False for the following.
   (a) $\frac{3}{4}$ of 2 ft > 9 in.   True / False
   (b) $1\frac{5}{12}$ years < 15 months   True / False

6. (a) Find the number of inches in 3 yards.
   (b) Find the number of centimeters in 4 kilometers.

7. Find the value of each of the following.
   (a) 2 km 740 m + 3 km 590 m   (b) 16 lb – 3 lb 10 oz
   (c) 1 h 25 min + 2 h 45 min   (d) 40 ft 5 in. – 6 ft 10 in.
   (e) 3 L 450 ml × 3   (f) 3 yd 2 ft × 12
   (g) 2 h 45 min × 3   (h) 3 h 20 min ÷ 2

155

Regular **reviews** in the Textbook provide consolidation of concepts learned.

GLOSSARY

Word	Meaning
equivalent fractions	**Equivalent fractions** are fractions that are equal in value. $\frac{1}{3} = \frac{2}{6} = \frac{3}{9}$
expanded form	We write the **expanded form** of the number 23,546 like this: $20,000 + 3,000 + 500 + 40 + 6$
factors	$2 \times 3 \times 4 = 12$ 2, 3 and 4 are **factors** of 12.
improper fractions	An **improper fraction** is a fraction that is equal to or greater than 1. $\frac{3}{3}$, $\frac{4}{3}$, $\frac{5}{3}$
mixed number	When we add a whole number and a fraction, the result is a **mixed number**. $1\frac{1}{2}$ and $3\frac{3}{4}$ are **mixed numbers**.
multiples	The first 5 **multiples** of 3 are 3, 6, 9, 12 and 15.
standard form	70,639 is how we write the **standard form** of the number seventy thousand, six hundred, thirty-nine.

158

The **glossary** effectively combines pictorial representation with simple mathematical definitions to provide a comprehensive reference guide for students.

CONTENTS

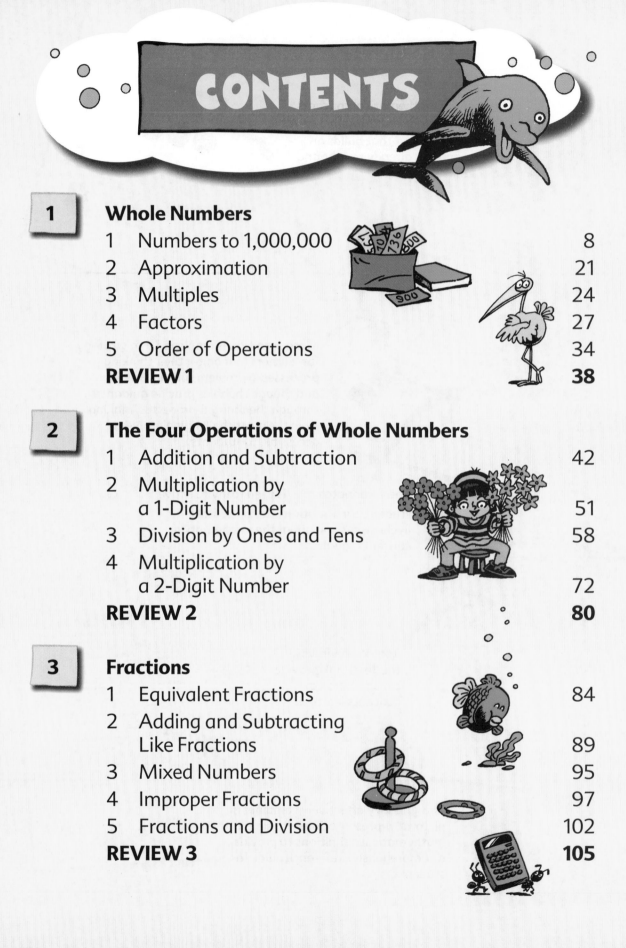

1 WHOLE NUMBERS

1 Numbers to 1,000,000

one cube
1

ten cubes
10

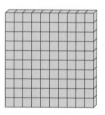

one hundred cubes
100

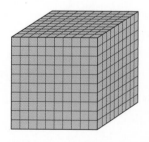

one thousand cubes
1,000

**ten thousand cubes
10,000**

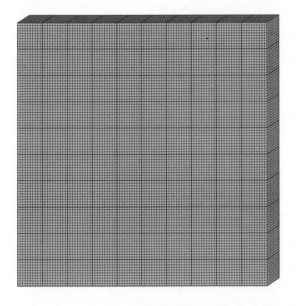

**one hundred thousand cubes
100,000**

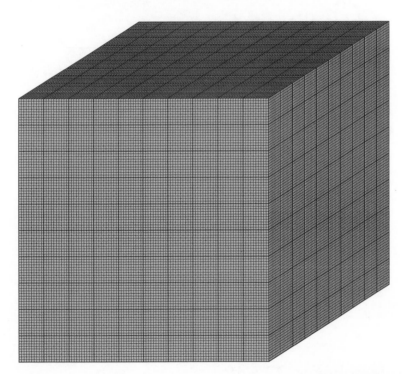

**one million cubes
1,000,000**

one million = a thousand thousands!

1. How many cubes are there altogether?

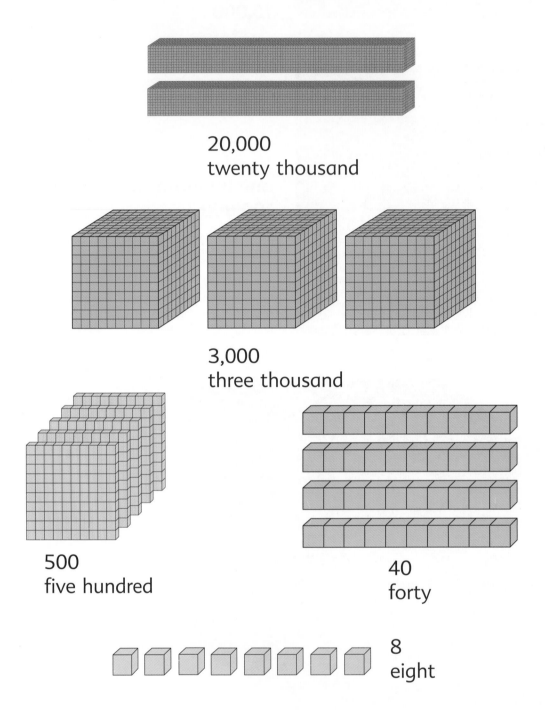

20,000
twenty thousand

3,000
three thousand

500
five hundred

40
forty

8
eight

The total number of cubes is 23,548.

23,548 is the **standard form** for twenty-three thousand, five hundred forty-eight.

2.

Ten thousands	Thousands	Hundreds	Tens	Ones
10,000 10,000	1,000 1,000 1,000	100 100 100 100 100	10 10 10 10	1 1 1 1 1 1
2	3	5	4	6

23,546 = 20,000 + 3,000 + 500 + 40 + 6
23,546 = 23,000 + 546
twenty-three thousand, five hundred forty-six

20,000 + 3,000 + 500 + 40 + 6 is the **expanded form** of 23,546.

Fill in the blanks.

23,546 = ◻ ten thousands ◻ thousands ◻ hundreds

◻ tens ◻ ones

3. Fill in the blanks.

   (a) 48,300 = 48 thousands, ◻ hundreds

   (b) 60,004 = 60 thousands, ◻ ones

4. Write the following in standard form.

   (a) 20 thousands, 8 hundreds
   (b) 35 thousands, 6 tens 2 ones
   (c) 88 thousands, 7 tens
   (d) 70 thousands, 3 ones
   (e) 80,000 + 4,000 + 90

5. A library has a collection of 124,936 books.

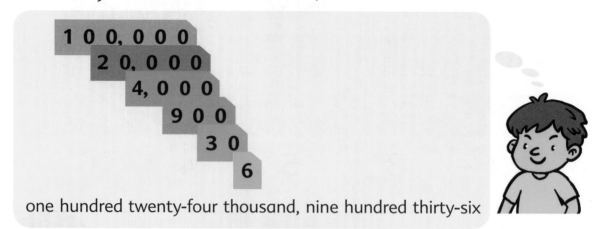

one hundred twenty-four thousand, nine hundred thirty-six

1 2 4, 9 3 6

Hundred thousands	Ten thousands	Thousands	Hundreds	Tens	Ones
1	2	4	9	3	6

Fill in the blanks.

124,936 = ☐ hundred thousand ☐ ten thousands

☐ thousands ☐ hundreds ☐ tens ☐ ones

6. Fill in the blanks.

(a) 451,400 = 451 thousands, ☐ hundreds

(b) 300,005 = ☐ thousands, ☐ ones

7. Write the following in standard form.

(a) 270 thousands, 6 hundreds
(b) 572 thousands, 6 tens 3 ones
(c) 300 thousands, 5 tens
(d) 800 thousands, 8 ones
(e) 400,000 + 4,000 + 40

8. Write the following in standard form.

    (a) eight thousand, twelve
    (b) forty-nine thousand, five hundred one
    (c) seventeen thousand, four
    (d) ninety thousand, ninety
    (e) four hundred one thousand, sixty-two
    (f) nine hundred seventy thousand, five hundred five
    (g) seven hundred thousand, nine

9. Write the following in words.

(a) 3,096	(b) 7,280	(c) 5,002
(d) 27,165	(e) 18,057	(f) 42,605
(g) 30,003	(h) 60,109	(i) 81,900
(j) 435,672	(k) 500,500	(l) 404,040
(m) 840,382	(n) 600,005	(o) 999,999

10. Write 805,620 in expanded form.

Exercise 1, pages 7–9

11. Use place-value cards to make a 5-digit number like this:

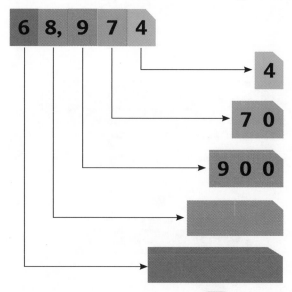

In 68,974, the digit **8** stands for ⬜ and the digit **6** stands for ⬜.

13

12. (a) Count the ten thousands, thousands, hundreds, tens and ones in this chart.

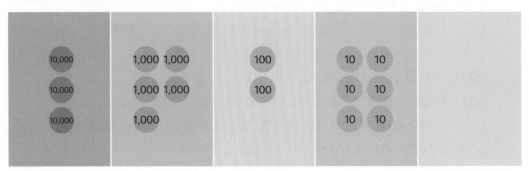

(b) What number is represented by the set of number discs?
(c) Which digit is in the hundreds place?
(d) Which digit is in the ten thousands place?
(e) What is the value of each digit in the number?

13. 26,345 people watched a soccer game at a stadium.
Fill in the blanks.

(a) Use a set of number discs to represent 26,345.

(b) 26,345 is ⬜ more than 26,000.

(c) 26,345 is ⬜ more than 6,345.

14.

Hundred thousands	Ten thousands	Thousands	Hundreds	Tens	Ones
6	8	2	3	0	7

⬇

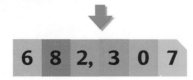

Fill in the blanks.

(a) In 682,307, the digit ⬜ is in the ten thousands place.

14

(b) The digit 6 is in the hundred thousands place.

Its value is ◯.

(c) The digit ◯ in the tens place shows that there are no tens.

(d) 682,307 is ◯ more than 82,307.

15. What does the digit 8 stand for in each of the following numbers?

(a) 16,**8**14   (b) **8**2,114   (c) 4**8**,050
(d) **8**26,042   (e) 92**8**,000   (f) 450,03**8**

16. (a) How many thousands are there in 48,243?

48,243 = 48,000 + 243

There are ◯ thousands in 48,243.

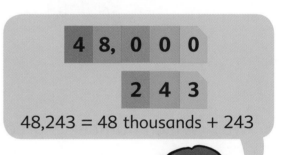

48,243 = 48 thousands + 243

(b) There are ◯ hundreds in 48,243.

17. (a) How many tens are there in 200,190?
(b) How many tens are there in 6,400?
(c) How many ten thousands are there in 415,010?

18. Find the value of each of the following.

(a) 36 thousands + 2 hundreds = ◯

(b) 14 hundreds + 8 tens = ◯

(c) 690 tens + 7 ones = ◯

(d) 92 ten thousands + 50 hundreds + 6 tens = ◯

Exercise 2, pages 10—12

19. What number does each letter represent?

(a)
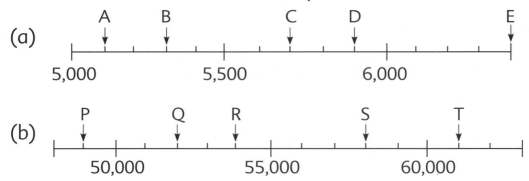

(b)
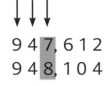

20. (a) Which number is smaller, 56,700 or 75,600?

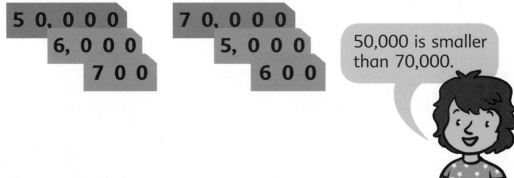

50,000 is smaller than 70,000.

(b) Which number is greater, 32,645 or 32,498?

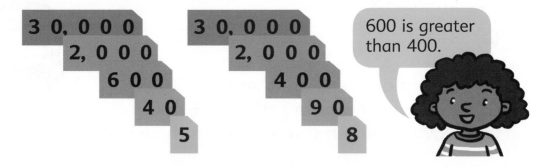

600 is greater than 400.

21. Which number is smaller, 947,612 or 948,104?

↓↓↓

9 4 7, 6 1 2
9 4 8, 1 0 4

First, compare the digits in the highest place, hundred thousands 9 = 9. The digits are the same. Then, compare the digits in each place after this until the two digits are different. In the thousands place, 7 < 8. So 94**7**,612 is smaller.

22. Which number is greater,
95,030 or 154,030?

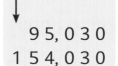

$$9\,5,0\,3\,0$$
$$1\,5\,4,0\,3\,0$$

23. Fill in each  with >, <,
or = to make each statement true.

(a) 35,045 ◯ 46,017   (b) 86,934 ◯ 86,925

(c) 257,490 ◯ 257,804 (d) 98,975 ◯ 432,674

24. Arrange the following numbers in increasing order.

(a) 53,760, 53,670, 56,370, 53,607
(b) 324,468, 342,468, 324,648
(c) 6,932, 69,320, 69,302, 9,623

Exercise 3, page 13

25. What are the missing numbers in the regular number
patterns in this number puzzle?

5,000	6,000	7,000				
					20,000	
29,500	29,600	29,700				30,100
			28,800			
24,230						
24,130			26,800		60,000	
24,030					70,000	
			24,800			
23,830	23,820	23,810				23,770
23,630		23,650		23,670		23,690

26. (a) What number is 10,000 more than 345,084?
(b) What number is 1,000 less than 945,006?
(c) What number is 100 less than 4,056?
(d) What number is 100 more than 79,930?
(e) What number is 10,000 less than 402,660?

27. Complete the following number patterns.

    (a) 83,002, 93,002, ⬜, ⬜, 123,002

    (b) 742,300, 742,200, 742,100, ⬜, ⬜, ⬜, 741,700

    (c) 287,512, 297,512, 298,512, 298,612, ⬜, ⬜

    (d) 44,067, 43,068, 42,069, ⬜, ⬜, ⬜

28. Create a regular number pattern that starts with 145,800 and increase each number by 100.

    145,800, ⬜, ⬜, ⬜, ⬜, ⬜

29. Create a regular number pattern that starts with 85,000 and decrease each number by 10.

    85,000, ⬜, ⬜, ⬜, ⬜, ⬜

30. The figures below form a pattern.

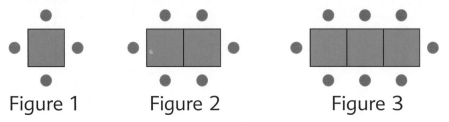

    Figure 1   Figure 2   Figure 3

    (a) Draw Figures 4 and 5.
    (b) Complete the table.

Figure number	1	2	3	4	5	6	7
Number of circles	4	6					

    (c) Look at the number of circles in each figure. What pattern do you notice in the numbers?

31. The figures below form a pattern.

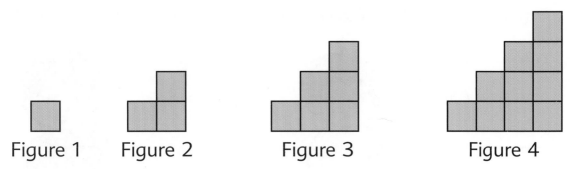

Figure 1   Figure 2   Figure 3   Figure 4

(a) Draw Figures 5 and 6.
(b) Complete the table.

Figure number	1	2	3	4	5	6	7	8
Number of squares	1	3	6					

(c) Look at the number of squares in each figure. What pattern do you notice in the numbers?

Exercise 4, pages 14—15

32. Find the value of each of the following.

(a) 6 + 8
(b) 6,000 + 8,000
(c) 60,000 + 80,000
(d) 27,000 + 4,000
(e) 15,000 − 6,000
(f) 310,000 − 50,000

27 + 4
∧
3 1

33. Find the missing number represented by n.

(a) $n + 70{,}000 = 620{,}000$

(b) $n - 2{,}000 = 32{,}000$

(c) $4{,}000 + n = 10{,}000$

(d) $51{,}000 - n = 42{,}000$

(e) $n + 690{,}000 = 694{,}000$

(f) $n - 60{,}000 = 850{,}000$

34. Create a regular number pattern that starts with 3 and multiply each number by 10. What do you notice?

3, ☐ , ☐ , ☐ , ☐

35. Find the value of each of the following.

(a) 4×3

(b) 40×3

(c) 400×3

(d) $4{,}000 \times 3$

(e) $40{,}000 \times 3$

(f) $7{,}000 \times 4$

(g) $36 \div 4$

(h) $3{,}600 \div 4$

(i) $360{,}000 \div 4$

(j) $30{,}000 \div 6$

36. Find the missing number represented by n.

(a) $50{,}000 \times n = 250{,}000$

(b) $720{,}000 \div n = 90{,}000$

$5 \times n = 25$
$25 \div 5 = n$

$72 \div n = 9$
$72 \div 9 = n$

(c) $n \times 4{,}000 = 32{,}000$

(d) $n \div 6 = 6{,}000$

20

Exercise 5, pages 16–18

2 Approximation

4,865 people watched a tennis game.

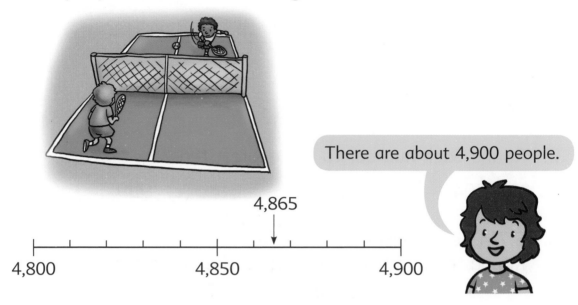

There are about 4,900 people.

4,865

```
|----|----|----|----|----|----|----|----|
4,800          4,850          4,900
```

Sally rounds 4,865 **to the nearest hundred**.

$$4,865 \approx 4,900$$

4,865 is **approximately** 4,900.

There are about 5,000 people.

4,865

```
|----|----|----|----|----|----|----|----|
4,000          4,500          5,000
```

Jenny rounds 4,865 **to the nearest thousand**.

$$4,865 \approx 5,000$$

4,865 is **approximately** 5,000.

Use the approximation sign ≈ to show rounding of numbers.

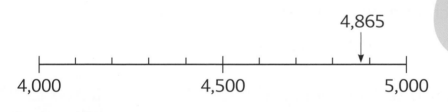

1. There are 487 pages in a book.
    Round the number of pages to the nearest ten.

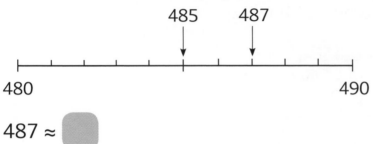

480   490

    $487 \approx$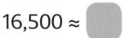

2. Round each number to the nearest ten.

    (a) 604   (b) 795   (c) 999

3. 5,714 people visited a book fair.
    Round the number of visitors to the nearest hundred.

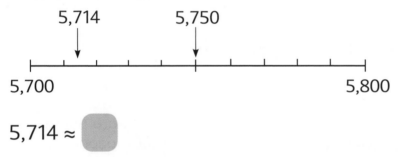

    5,700   5,800

    $5,714 \approx$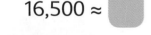

4. Round each number to the nearest hundred.

    (a) 3,650   (b) 6,047   (c) 4,995

5. Round 16,500 to the nearest thousand.

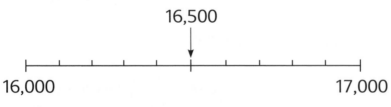

    16,500 is halfway between 16,000 and 17,000.
    We take 17,000 as the nearest thousand.

    16,000   17,000

    $16,500 \approx$

6. Round each number to the nearest thousand.

    (a) 23,490   (b) 54,550   (c) 39,900

To round a number to the nearest ten thousand, we can look at the digit in the thousands place. If it is 5 or greater than 5, we round up. If it is smaller than 5, we round down.

7. Round each number to the nearest ten thousand.

(a) 49,287 ≈ 50,000

(b) 73,501 ≈

(c) 804,390 ≈

(d) 129,500 ≈

8. Round 836,529 to the nearest hundred thousand.

> The digit 8 is in the hundred thousands place.
>
> **8**36,529
>
> What digit is in the next lower place?
>
> 8**3**6,529
>
> Do we round up or down?

836,529 is   when it is rounded to the nearest hundred thousand.

9. What is 796,030 rounded to the nearest hundred thousand?

> We round up. 796,030 rounded to the nearest hundred thousand is 800,000.

10. Round each number to the nearest thousand, ten thousand, and hundred thousand.

(a) 243,700   (b) 138,465   (c) 567,501
(d) 349,999   (e) 99,501   (f) 651,491

Exercise 6, pages 19—20

③ Multiples

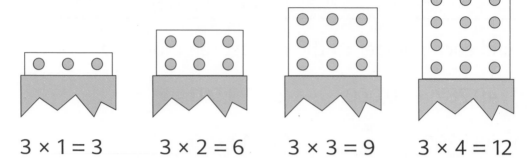

$3 \times 1 = 3$ $3 \times 2 = 6$ $3 \times 3 = 9$ $3 \times 4 = 12$

3, 6, 9 and 12 are **multiples** of 3.

A multiple of 3 can be expressed as the **product** of 3 and a whole number.

Name other multiples of 3.

List the first four multiples of 5.

$5 \times 1 = 5$
$5 \times 2 = 10$
$5 \times 3 = 15$
$5 \times 4 = 20$

Name other multiples of 5.

Name some multiples of 10.

1. (a) Create a regular number pattern that starts with 2 and increase each number by 2.

Multiples of 2 are even numbers.

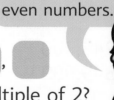

2, 4, , , , , , ,

Is each number in the pattern a multiple of 2?

(b) Create a regular number pattern that starts with 1 and increase each number by 2.

1, 3, [ ], [ ], [ ], [ ], [ ], [ ], [ ]

Is each number in the pattern a multiple of 2?

2. In the table below, the multiples of 2 are circled and the multiples of 5 are crossed out.

1	②	3	④	~~5~~	⑥	7	⑧	9	⑩̶
11	⑫	13	⑭	~~15~~	⑯	17	⑱	19	⑳̶
21	㉒	23	㉔	~~25~~	㉖	27	㉘	29	㉚̶
31	㉜	33	㉞	~~35~~	㊱	37	㊳	39	㊵̶
41	㊷	43	㊹	~~45~~	㊻	47	㊽	49	㊿̶
51	㋂	53	㋄	~~55~~	㋆	57	㋈	59	㋊̶
61	㋌	63	㋎	~~65~~	㋐	67	㋒	69	㋔̶
71	㋖	73	㋘	~~75~~	㋚	77	㋜	79	㋞̶
81	㋠	83	㋢	~~85~~	㋤	87	㋦	89	㋨̶
91	㋪	93	㋬	~~95~~	㋮	97	㋰	99	̶100̶

Fill in the blanks.

(a) When a number is a multiple of 2,
its ones digit is 0, 2, [ ], [ ], or [ ].

(b) When a number is a multiple of 5,
its ones digit is [ ], or [ ].

25

3. (a) List the first 10 multiples of 3.
   (b) Find the sum of the digits of each number greater than 9. Is the sum a multiple of 3?
   (c) List some other multiples of 3. Find the sum of their digits.
   (d) Is 76 a multiple of 3?
   (e) Is 114 a multiple of 3?

4. (a) Complete the multiplication table below.

×	1	2	3	4	5	6	7	8	9	10
3										
9										

   (b) Compare each multiple of 9 to the multiple of 3 in the same column. What do you notice?
   (c) Find the sum of the digits for each multiple of 9. What do you notice?
   (d) Is 114 a multiple of 9?

5. Find the next six numbers in each of the following regular number patterns.
   (a) 4, 8, 12, 16, ⬜ , ⬜ , ⬜ , ⬜ , ⬜ , ⬜
   (b) 6, 12, 18, 24, ⬜ , ⬜ , ⬜ , ⬜ , ⬜ , ⬜
   (c) Find a rule for multiples of 6 and test your rule with other numbers.
   (d) Can you find a rule for multiples of 4?

6. (a) Is 12 a multiple of 2?   (b) Is 12 a multiple of 3?
   (c) Is 12 a multiple of 4?   (d) Is 12 a multiple of 5?
   (e) Is 12 a multiple of 6?

Exercise 7, pages 21–22

4 Factors

factor × factor = product

$3 \times 4 = 12$

12 is the product of 3 and 4.

12 is a multiple of 3. It is also a multiple of 4.

3 and 4 are **factors** of 12.

$2 \times 3 \times 4 = 24$

24 is the **product** of 2, 3 and 4.
2, 3 and 4 are **factors** of 24.

1.  $1 \times 6 = 6$

   $2 \times 3 = 6$

We can write some numbers as a product of factors in different ways.

1, 2, ⬜ and ⬜ are factors of 6.

Is 4 a factor of 6?

Is 5 a factor of 6?

2.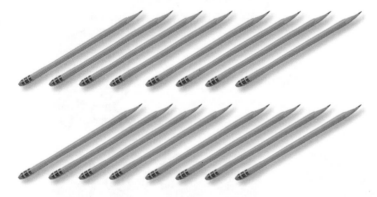

2 and 8 are factors of 16.
Name other factors of 16.

⬜ $\times 4 = 16$

$2 \times 8 = 16$

3.

$1 \times 5 = 5$

5 has only two factors, 1 and itself, 5.

Can I make more than one equal row?

A number greater than 1 is a **composite number** if it has at least two factors that are not 1. The factors of 16 are 1, 2, 4, 8 and 16. So, 16 is a composite number.

A number greater than 1 is called a **prime number** if it has exactly two factors, 1 and the number itself. So, 5 is a prime number.

4. Find the factors of each number.
   Which numbers are prime numbers?

   (a) 7   (b) 9   (c) 3   (d) 18
   (e) 11   (f) 15   (g) 10   (h) 13

1 is neither a prime number nor a composite number.

5. (a) Which of the following numbers have 2 as a factor?

   8,   10,   15,   24

   (b) Which of the following numbers have 5 as a factor?

   15,   20,   25,   32

Exercise 8, pages 23—24

6. (a) Is 3 a factor of 21?

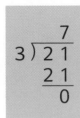

21 can be divided by 3 exactly. So 3 is a factor of 21.

(b) Is 3 a factor of 26?

26 cannot be divided by 3 exactly. So 3 is not a factor of 26.

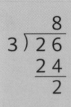

(c) Determine if 3 is a factor of 84 without using division. Then check your answer with division.

7. (a) Is 2 a factor of 98?   (b) Is 4 a factor of 98?

8. Find the missing factors.

   (a) $28 = 7 \times$ ☐   (b) $40 = 5 \times$ ☐   (c) $72 = 8 \times$ ☐

   (d) $81 = 9 \times$ ☐   (e) $63 = 9 \times$ ☐   (f) $56 = 7 \times$ ☐

9. (a) Is 4 a factor of 60?

   (b) Is 4 a factor of 84?

   (c) Is 4 a **common factor** of 60 and 84?

10. (a) Is 5 a common factor of 75 and 80?

    (b) Is 8 a common factor of 72 and 96?

11. The multiples of 4 are

4,   8,   **12**,   16,   20,   24,   28,   ...

The multiples of 6 are

6,   **12**,   18,   24,   30,   36,   42,   ...

12 is a **common multiple** of 4 and 6.

Name the next two common multiples of 4 and 6.

There is more than one common multiple of 4 and 6.

12. (a) Which of the following numbers are common factors of 36 and 63?

| 3 | 4 | 6 | 9 | 12 |

(b) Which of the following numbers are common multiples of 6 and 9?

| 9 | 18 | 27 | 36 | 45 |

13. Find a common multiple of 3 and 5.

The multiples of 5 are 5, 10, 15, 20, ...
15 is also a multiple of 3.

14. Find the factors of 32.

   $32 = 1 \times 32$
   $32 = 2 \times 16$
   $32 = 4 \times 8$

   The factors of 32 are 1, 2, , , and .

15. Find the factors of 48.

   $48 = 1 \times 48$

   $48 = 2 \times$

   $48 = 3 \times$

   $48 = 4 \times$

   $48 = 6 \times$

   The factors of 48 are 1, 2, 3, 4, 6, , , , and 48.

16. Find the factors of 100.

   $100 = 1 \times 100$
   $= 2 \times 50$
   $= 4 \times 25$
   $= ...$

17. Find the factors of each number.

   (a) 40   (b) 50   (c) 75   (d) 80

18. Find the missing factors.

$12 = \quad 4 \times 3$

$\quad = \mathbf{2} \times \mathbf{2} \times 3$

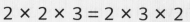

$2 \times 2 \times 3 = 2 \times 3 \times 2$

$12 = \mathbf{6} \times 2$

$\quad = \mathbf{2} \times \boxed{} \times 2$

$24 = \mathbf{12} \times 2$

$\quad = \boxed{} \times \mathbf{3} \times 2$

$\quad = \mathbf{2} \times \boxed{} \times \mathbf{3} \times 2$

$24 = 12 \times \boxed{}$

$\quad = 6 \times \boxed{} \times 2$

$\quad = 3 \times \boxed{} \times 2 \times 2$

$\quad = 3 \times 2 \times \boxed{}$

$\quad = 3 \times \boxed{}$

19. Find the missing factors represented by n.

(a) $30 = 5 \times 2 \times n$ (b) $16 = 4 \times n \times 2$
(c) $35 \times 3 = 5 \times n \times 3$ (d) $25 \times 24 = 25 \times 4 \times n$
(e) $4 \times 24 = 8 \times n$ (f) $64 \times 2 = n \times 4$

Exercise 9, pages 25–28

5 Order of Operations

Matthew arranges his stamps on two pages of his stamp album like this:

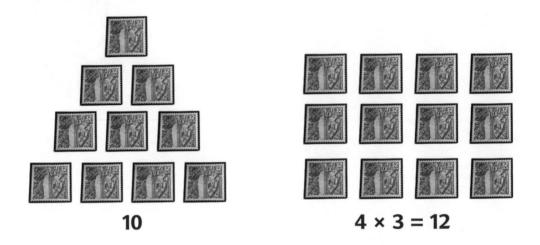

10   **4 × 3 = 12**

Then he finds the total number of stamps.

Do multiplication first.

10 + 4 × 3 = 10 + 12
            = 22

There are 22 stamps altogether.

Order of Operations:
Do multiplication or division from left to right, then addition or subtraction from left to right.

---

1. Find the value of each of the following.

    (a) 12 + 8 − 10   (b) 60 − 12 − 24   (c) 31 − 19 + 11
    (d) 43 + 16 − 27   (e) 64 + 26 + 57   (f) 90 − 12 + 21
    (g) 15 + 19 − 5   (h) 61 − 19 − 11   (i) 58 − 25 + 42

2. Find the value of each of the following.

    (a) 2 × 4 × 8   (b) 60 ÷ 4 ÷ 3   (c) 54 ÷ 6 × 3
    (d) 4 × 5 × 6   (e) 72 ÷ 6 ÷ 4   (f) 4 × 20 ÷ 8
    (g) 4 × 2 × 20   (h) 64 ÷ 8 ÷ 8   (i) 9 × 8 ÷ 9

> An **expression** has numbers and operation signs (+, −, ×, ÷) grouped together which can be evaluated as a number. It does not have an equal sign.

3. Find the value of each expression.

    (a) 9 + 3 × 6   (b) 27 − 12 ÷ 3
    (c) 4 + 5 × 8   (d) 80 − 5 × 10
    (e) 54 − 48 ÷ 6   (f) 9 + 81 ÷ 9
    (g) 56 − 8 × 5 + 4   (h) 70 + 40 ÷ 5 × 4
    (i) 96 ÷ 8 − 6 × 2   (j) 6 + 54 ÷ 9 × 2
    (k) 49 − 45 ÷ 5 × 3   (l) 62 + 42 ÷ 7 − 6

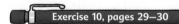
Exercise 10, pages 29–30

4. Find the value of 27 − 2 × (3 + 5).

    27 − 2 × **(3 + 5)**
    = 27 − 2 × **8**

    =

> Do what is in the parentheses first.

5. Find the value of each of the following.

    (a) 9 + (36 + 16)   (b) 100 − (87 − 13)
    (c) 99 − (87 + 12)   (d) 18 × (5 × 2)
    (e) 49 ÷ (7 × 7)   (f) 100 × (27 ÷ 9)

6. Find the value of each of the following.

    (a) $60 \div (4 + 8)$ (b) $20 - 2 \times (18 \div 6)$

    (c) $25 + (5 + 7) \div 3$ (d) $(22 + 10) \div 8 \times 5$

    (e) $(50 - 42) \div 2 \times 7$ (f) $100 \div 10 \times (4 + 6)$

Exercise 11, pages 31–32

7. (a) Shawna had $20. She spent $8 on a toy and $5 on a book. How much money does she have now?

        Shawna spent $8 + $5.
        We can write the expression
        $20 − ($8 + $5).
        Find how much money she had left.

   (b) Paul had $20 and spent $8. He then made $5 more. How much money does he have now?

        We can write the expression
        ($20 − $8) + $5.
        How much money does he have now?

   (c) Is $20 − ($8 + $5) the same as ($20 − $8) + $5?

8. Mrs. Harris bought 5 bags of apples and 2 boxes of oranges. There were 8 apples in each bag and 16 oranges in each box.

    (a) Write an expression for how many pieces of fruit she bought altogether, using the numbers 2, 5, 8 and 16 only.

    (b) How many pieces of fruit did she buy altogether?

9. This equation is true.

   $8 = 2 \times 4$

   (a) Add 10 to both sides. Is the equation still true?
       $8 + 10 = (2 \times 4) + 10$

   (b) Add 10 to one side and 2×5 to the other side.
       Is the equation still true?
       $8 + 10 = (2 \times 4) + (2 \times 5)$

   (c) Multiply both sides by 10. Is the equation still true?
       $8 \times 10 = (2 \times 4) \times 10$

   (d) Multiply one side by 10 and the other side by $(5 + 5)$.
       Is the equation still true?

       $8 \times 10 = 2 \times 4 \times (5 + 5)$

       When we add or multiply both sides of an equation by the same number, the two sides stay equal.

10. Find the number that goes in each ▢ to make the equation true.

    (a) $24 + (15 - 4) = \boxed{} + 11$

    (b) $(4 + 5) \times (3 + 7) = \boxed{} \times 10$

    (c) $100 \times (10 \div 5) = \boxed{} \times 2$

    (d) $(14 + 10) \div 2 \times 3 = \boxed{} \times 3$

Exercise 12, pages 33–34

REVIEW 1

1. Which of the following is equal to 308,274?

    (A) 300,000 + 80,000 + 2,000 + 70 + 4
    (B) 300,000 + 80,000 + 200 + 70 + 4
    (C) 300,000 + 8,000 + 200 + 70 + 4
    (D) 30,000 + 8,000 + 200 + 70 + 4

2. 56,000 − 7,000 = _____.

    (A) 49 ones   (B) 49 tens
    (C) 49 hundreds   (D) 49 thousands

3. How many thousands are there in 913,913?

    (A) 39   (B) 913   (C) 13   (D) 3

4. 875,194 is _____ more than 5,194.

    (A) 87   (B) 8,700   (C) 87,000   (D) 870,000

5. What number does A represent?

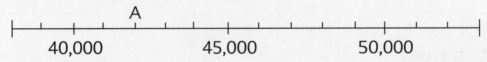

    (A) 41,000 (B) 42,000 (C) 43,000 (D) 44,000

6. Select True or False for the following.

    (a) 52 thousands + 8 hundreds = 52,800   True / False
    (b) 690 tens + 3 ones = 693   True / False

7. Select True or False for the following.

    (a) 21,395 + 10,000 < 31,395 − 10,000   True / False
    (b) 1,000,000 > 869,901 + 100,000   True / False

8. Write the following in standard form.

   (a) 13 thousands, 7 hundreds 3 tens
   (b) 27 thousands, 8 tens 9 ones
   (c) 1 million
   (d) two hundred four thousand, eight hundred three
   (e) five hundred sixty thousand, thirteen

9. Write the following in words.

   (a) 15,780   (b) 306,903   (c) 20,004

10. What is the value of the digit 6 in each of the following?

    (a) **6**54,020   (b) 934,**6**20   (c) **6**0,143

11. Complete the following number patterns.

    (a) 5,780, 5,880, ⬜, ⬜, 6,180

    (b) 82,465, 92,465, ⬜, ⬜, 122,465

    (c) 502,346, 402,346, 302,346, ⬜, ⬜

12.

    Figure 1   Figure 2   Figure 3

    (a) Draw Figures 4 and 5.
    (b) Complete the table.

Figure number	1	2	3	4	5	6	7	8
Number of squares								

    (c) Look at the number of squares.
        What pattern do you notice in the numbers?

13. Write >, < or = in place of each ⬤ to make the equations true.

   (a) 14,012 ⬤ 41,102   (b) 412,613 ⬤ 412,632

   (c) 56,375 ⬤ 6,300 + 88   (d) 700,000 ⬤ 700 × 1,000

   (e) 16,000 ÷ 4 ⬤ 400   (f) 60,000 × 2 ⬤ 40,000 × 3

14. Find the missing number represented by n.

   (a) $n \times 6,000 = 48,000$ (b) $490,000 \div n = 70,000$
   (c) $30,000 \times n = 270,000$ (d) $n \div 5,000 = 7$

15. Arrange the following numbers in decreasing order.

   (a) 30,601, 30,061, 30,160, 300,160
   (b) 29,999, 90,000, 20,990, 29,909

16. Mount Everest is the highest mountain in the world.
    It is 29,028 ft high.
    Round this height to the nearest thousand ft.

17. 136,246 people attended an arts festival. Round the number of people to the nearest ten thousand.

18. Round the number 940,052 to

   (a) the nearest hundred thousand,
   (b) the nearest ten thousand,
   (c) the nearest thousand.

19. (a) Is 3 a factor of 28?   (b) Is 5 a factor of 60?
    (c) Is 6 a factor of 80?   (d) Is 5 a factor of 92?
    (e) Is 4 a factor of 100?

20. What are the factors of 31?

21. Does every number that has 9 as a factor also have

    (a) 3 as a factor?   (b) 6 as a factor?

22. Find a number that satisfies the conditions for each statement.

    (a) Less than 60, and a common multiple of 10 and 15.
    (b) Greater than 10, and a common factor of 28 and 42.
    (c) Less than 100, not 35, and a common multiple of 5 and 7.
    (d) Less than 80, and a multiple of 3, 4, 5, and 10.

23. Find the missing factors represented by n.

    (a) $35 \times 3 = 5 \times n \times 3$ (b) $25 \times 24 = 25 \times 4 \times n$
    (c) $4 \times 24 = 8 \times n$ (d) $64 \times 2 = n \times 4$

24. Find the value of each of the following expressions.

    (a) $4 + 32 \div 8$ (b) $6 \times (22 - 12)$
    (c) $40 - (3 \times 12) \div 6$ (d) $60 \div 10 - (4 + 2)$

25. What is the greatest whole number that can be placed in
    each ⬚ to make the expression true?

    (a) $3 \times$ ⬚ < 20 (b) $4 \times$ ⬚ < 25

    (c) $6 \times$ ⬚ < 50 (d) $7 \times$ ⬚ < 50

    (e) $8 \times$ ⬚ < 66 (f) $9 \times$ ⬚ < 42

    (g) $5 +$ ⬚ < 20 (h) ⬚ $- 8 < 20$

26. Mr. Torres's farm produces about 44,400 eggs each month.
    Which is the possible number of eggs, 44,451 or 44,351? Why?

27. Are all prime numbers odd numbers? Explain.

Review 1, pages 35–39

2 THE FOUR OPERATIONS OF WHOLE NUMBERS

1 Addition and Subtraction

There are 3,402 boys at a parade.
There are 987 more boys than girls.

(a) How many girls are there?

There are more boys than girls.

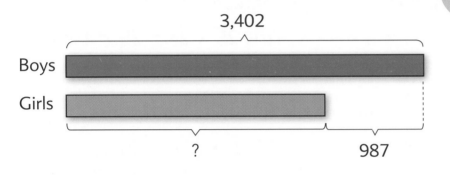

3,402 − 987 = 2,415

$$\begin{array}{r} \overset{2}{\cancel{3}}\overset{13}{\cancel{4}}\overset{9}{\cancel{0}}\overset{12}{\cancel{2}} \\ -\quad 9\,8\,7 \\ \hline 2,4\,1\,5 \end{array}$$

There are 2,415 girls.

We can check the answer:
Does 2,415 + 987 = 3,402?

(b) How many children are there altogether?

3,402 + 2,415 = 5,817

$$\begin{array}{r} 3,4\,0\,2 \\ +\quad 2,4\,1\,5 \\ \hline 5,8\,1\,7 \end{array}$$

There are 5,817 children.

There are 3,402 boys.
There are 2,415 girls.
There are 5,817 children altogether.

The **sum** of 3,402 and 2,415 is 5,817.

There are 3,402 boys.
There are 2,415 girls.
There are 987 more boys than girls.

The **difference** between 3,402 and 2,415 is 987.

1. Find the sum of 864 and 659.

   864 + 659 = ⬜

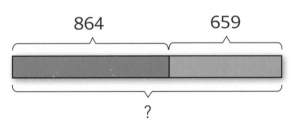

2. Find the difference between 674 and 467.

   674 − 467 = ⬜

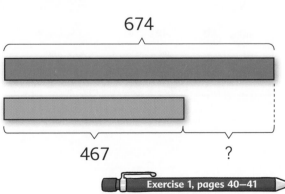

Exercise 1, pages 40—41

3. When 376 is subtracted from a number, the answer is 825. Find the number.

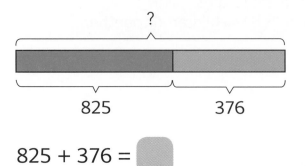

?

825   376

825 + 376 = ☐

☐ − 376 = 825

4. What number must be added to 462 to give the answer 1,000?

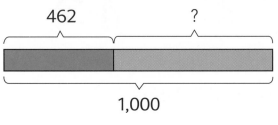

462   ?

1,000

1,000 − 462 = ☐

462 + ☐ = 1,000

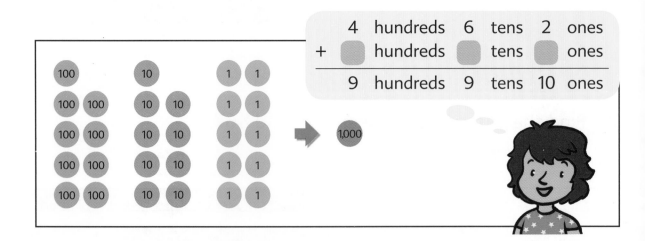

	4	hundreds	6	tens	2	ones
+	☐	hundreds	☐	tens	☐	ones
	9	hundreds	9	tens	10	ones

5. Find the value of each of the following.

   (a) 10 – 7   (b) 100 – 7   (c) 1,000 – 7
   (d) 100 – 26   (e) 1,000 – 26   (f) 1,000 – 260

 Exercise 2, pages 42–43

6. Add 574 and 998.

Method 1:	Method 2:
$$\begin{array}{r} \overset{1}{5}\overset{1}{7}4 \\ +\ 998 \\ \hline 1,572 \end{array}$$	998, 1,000, 2 (number bond) 574 + 1,000 = 1,574 1,574 – 2 = 1,572 So, 574 + 998 = 1,572

7. Subtract 998 from 3,221.

Method 1:	Method 2:
$$\begin{array}{r} \overset{2}{3},\overset{11}{2}\overset{11}{2}\overset{11}{1} \\ -\ \ 998 \\ \hline 2,223 \end{array}$$	3,221 – 1,000 = 2,221 2,221 + 2 = 2,223 So, 3,221 – 998 = 2,223

8. Find the value of each of the following.

   (a) 2,436 + 9   (b) 2,436 + 99   (c) 2,436 + 999
   (d) 2,436 – 9   (e) 2,436 – 99   (f) 2,436 – 999

 Exercise 3, pages 44–45

9. Add 746 and 58.

Method 1:

$$\begin{array}{r} \overset{1}{7}\overset{1}{4}6 \\ +58 \\ \hline 804 \end{array}$$

Method 2:

$$746 + 58$$

$$744 \quad 2$$

$$58 + 2 = 60$$

$$746 + 58 = 744 + 60$$

$$= 804$$

10. Subtract 49 from 603.

Method 1:

$$\begin{array}{r} \overset{5}{6}\overset{9}{0}\overset{13}{3} \\ -49 \\ \hline 554 \end{array}$$

Method 2:

$$603 - 49$$

$$553 \quad 50$$

$$50 - 49 = 1$$

$$603 - 49 = 553 + 1$$

$$= 554$$

11. Add 2,454 and 708.

$$2,454 \xrightarrow{+700} \boxed{} \xrightarrow{+8} \boxed{}$$

12. Subtract 602 from 3,541.

$$3,541 \xrightarrow{-600} \boxed{} \xrightarrow{-2} \boxed{}$$

13. Find the value of each of the following.

    (a) 37 + 48   (b) 54 − 39   (c) 95 − 18
    (d) 489 + 57   (e) 843 − 78   (f) 492 + 79

 Exercise 4, pages 46–47

14. Round each number to the nearest hundred.  712 → 700
    Then, estimate the value of 712 + 492.   492 → 500

    700 + 500 =

    The value of 712 + 492 is about .

15. Estimate the value of 578 + 67.

    578 → 600   578 → 580
    67 → 70   67 → 70
    The value of 578 + 67   The value of 578 + 67
    is about   .   is about   .

 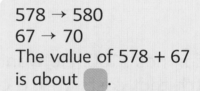

16. Estimate the value of each of the following.

    (a) 384 + 296   (b) 537 + 89   (c) 2,987 + 789
    (d) 716 − 382   (e) 983 − 29   (f) 8,817 − 438

17. Estimate the value of 786 − 297 + 518.

Round each number to the nearest hundred.
786 → 800
297 → 300
518 → 500

800 − 300 + 500 = ◯

The value of 786 − 297 + 518 is about ◯.

18. Estimate the value of each of the following.

(a) 418 + 293 + 108   (b) 784 + 617 + 399
(c) 814 + 208 − 587   (d) 1,205 − 489 − 596
(e) 834 + 87 + 538   (f) 1,195 + 896 + 79
(g) 847 − 37 − 282   (h) 7,478 − 4,802 − 649

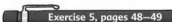
Exercise 5, pages 48—49

19. Jordan has $100. He wants to buy a watch that costs $39, a calculator that costs $14 and a book that costs $19. Does he have enough money?

I can use an estimate to see if I have enough money. I am going to round up the prices of the items.

$40 + $20 + $20 = ◯

He ◯ enough money.

20. Lisa will win a prize if she sells 250 boxes of cookies. She sells 84 boxes in February and 62 boxes in March. How many more boxes does she have to sell to get the prize?

We want to find an exact number.

$250 - 84 - 62 = \boxed{}$

She has to sell $\boxed{}$ more boxes to get the prize.

21. There were 6,020 spectators at a football game. 3,860 of them were men, 2,020 were women and the rest were children. How many children were there?

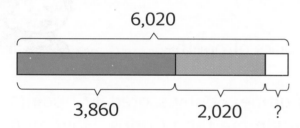

6,020

3,860   2,020   ?

$6,020 - 3,860 - 2,020 = \boxed{}$

There were $\boxed{}$ children.

22. A farmer has 1,025 ducks. He has 295 more chickens than ducks. How many chickens and ducks does he have altogether?

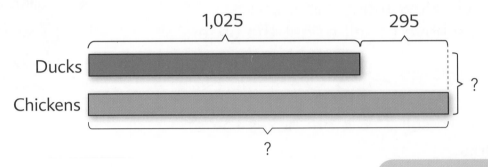

1,025

295

Ducks

Chickens

?

?

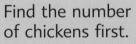

Find the number of chickens first.

1,025 + 295 = 1,320

He has 1,320 chickens.

1,025 + 1,320 =

He has ⬜ chickens and ducks altogether.

23. Abe scored 643 points in a game. Benny scored 172 points more than Abe and 84 points more than Carlos. How many points did the three boys score altogether?

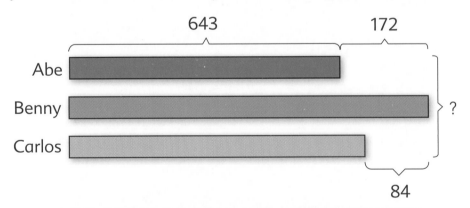

643

172

Abe

Benny

?

Carlos

84

How many points did Benny score?
How many points did Carlos score?
How many points did they score altogether?

They scored points altogether.

Exercise 6, pages 50—51

2 Multiplication by a 1-Digit Number

Sean has 135 US stamps. He has 3 times as many foreign stamps as US stamps.

How many stamps does he have altogether?

There are more foreign stamps than US stamps.

$$135 \times 4 = 540$$

$$\begin{array}{r} 1\,3\,5 \\ \times 4 \\ \hline 5\,4\,0 \end{array}$$

He has 540 stamps altogether.

Multiply 135 by 4.

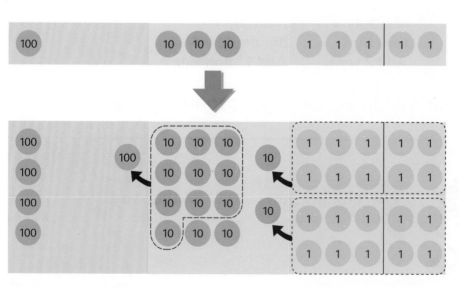

$$100 \times 4 = 400 \quad 30 \times 4 = 120 \quad 5 \times 4 = 20$$

```
  100
   30   × 4
     5
```

```
   1 3 5
 ×     4
 ─────────
      2 0  ← 5 × 4
    1 2 0  ← 30 × 4
    4 0 0  ← 100 × 4
 ─────────
```

135 × 4 = (100 × 4) + (30 × 4) + (5 × 4)

= 400 + 120 + 20

=

Here is another way to show multiplication.

```
    2              1 2            1 2
  1 3 5          1 3 5          1 3 5
×     4    ➡    ×     4    ➡    ×     4
─────────       ─────────       ─────────
      0              4 0          5 4 0
```

Multiply 5 ones by 4.

Multiply 3 tens by 4. Add 2 tens.

Multiply 1 hundred by 4. Add 1 hundred.

When 135 is multiplied by 4, the **product** is 540.

We can also show our work this way.

	100	30	5
4	100 × 4 = 400	30 × 4 = 120	5 × 4 = 20

```
    4 0 0
    1 2 0
 +    2 0
 ─────────
```

52

1. Multiply 407 by 3.

$$\begin{array}{r} 407 \\ \times \quad 3 \\ \hline \square \\ \hline \end{array}$$

	400	0	7
3	400 × 3 = ☐	0 × 3 = ☐	7 × 3 = ☐

$$\begin{array}{r} \square \\ + \ \square \\ \hline \square \\ \hline \end{array}$$

2. Multiply.

(a) 53 × 7 (b) 67 × 9 (c) 5 × 86
(d) 720 × 4 (e) 604 × 8 (f) 6 × 495

3. Estimate the value of 492 × 8.

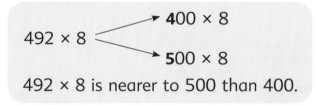

492 × 8 → **4**00 × 8
492 × 8 → **5**00 × 8

492 × 8 is nearer to 500 than 400.

500 × 8 = ☐

$$\begin{array}{r} 492 \\ \times \quad 8 \\ \hline 3,936 \\ \hline \end{array}$$

Is the exact answer close to the estimated answer?

4. Estimate and then multiply.

(a) 78 × 7 (b) 83 × 8 (c) 98 × 9
(d) 314 × 6 (e) 895 × 9 (f) 507 × 8

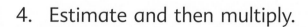

Exercise 7, pages 52–54

5. $3 \times 1{,}612 =$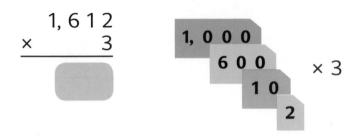

$$\begin{array}{r} 1{,}6\,1\,2 \\ \times \qquad 3 \\ \hline \end{array}$$

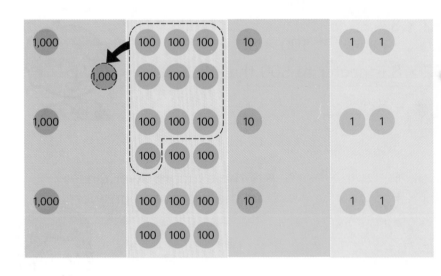

× 3

	1,000	600	10	2
3	1,000 × 3 = 3,000	600 × 3 = 1,800	10 × 3 = 30	2 × 3 = 6

$1{,}612 \times 3$
$= 3{,}000 + 1{,}800 + 30 + 6$
$= 4{,}836$

Multiply the ones by 3.

$$\begin{array}{r} 1{,}6\,1\,2 \\ \times \qquad 3 \\ \hline 6 \end{array}$$

Multiply the tens by 3.

$$\begin{array}{r} 1{,}6\,1\,2 \\ \times \qquad 3 \\ \hline 3\,6 \end{array}$$

Multiply the hundreds by 3.

$$\begin{array}{r} {}^{1}\,1{,}6\,1\,2 \\ \times \qquad 3 \\ \hline 8\,3\,6 \end{array}$$

Multiply the thousands by 3.

$$\begin{array}{r} {}^{1}\,1{,}6\,1\,2 \\ \times \qquad 3 \\ \hline 4{,}8\,3\,6 \end{array}$$

6. Multiply 3,726 by 5.

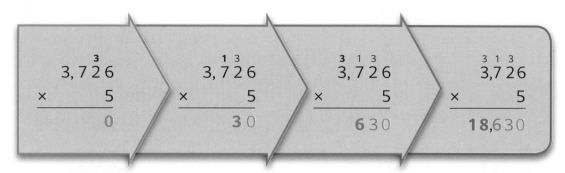

$$\begin{array}{r}\overset{\overset{3}{}}{3,726}\\ \times5\\\hline 0\end{array}$$ > $$\begin{array}{r}\overset{\overset{1}{}\overset{3}{}}{3,726}\\ \times5\\\hline 30\end{array}$$ > $$\begin{array}{r}\overset{\overset{3}{}\overset{1}{}\overset{3}{}}{3,726}\\ \times5\\\hline 630\end{array}$$ > $$\begin{array}{r}\overset{\overset{3}{}\overset{1}{}\overset{3}{}}{3,726}\\ \times5\\\hline 18,630\end{array}$$

7. Multiply.

(a) $2{,}950 \times 6 = \boxed{}$

	2,000	900	50
6	2,000 × 6 = $\boxed{}$	900 × 6 = $\boxed{}$	50 × 6 = $\boxed{}$

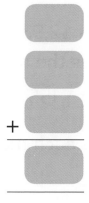

$$\begin{array}{r}\boxed{}\\ \boxed{}\\ +\boxed{}\\\hline \boxed{}\end{array}$$

(b) $8 \times 3{,}245 = \boxed{}$

$$\begin{array}{r}3{,}245\\ \times8\\\hline \boxed{}\end{array}$$

8. Estimate the value of 6,218 × 4.

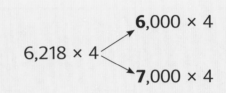

6,218 × 4 ⟨
→ **6,000** × 4
→ **7,000** × 4

6,218 is nearer to 6,000 than to 7,000.

6,000 × 4 = ◻

The value of 6,218 × 4 is about ◻.

9. Estimate and then multiply.

(a) 4,076 × 5 (b) 4,317 × 8 (c) 2,050 × 9
(d) 7 × 6,931 (e) 9 × 2,173 (f) 6 × 3,840

Exercise 8, page 55

10. Mr. Cohen earns $2,935 a month. If he spends $1,780 each month and saves the rest, how much will he save in 6 months?

2,935 − 1,780 = 1,155

He saves $1,155 each month.

First, find the amount Mr. Cohen saves each month.

1,155 × 6 = ◻

He will save $◻ in 6 months.

11. David bought 6 cameras at $1,340 each. Then he bought another 8 cameras at $1,248 each. How much did he spend altogether?

$1,340 \times 6 = 8,040$

He spent $8,040 on the first 6 cameras.

First, find the total amount David spent on the first 6 cameras. Then, find the total amount he spent on the next 8 cameras.

$1,248 \times 8 = 9,984$

He spent $9,984 on the next 8 cameras.

$8,040 + 9,984 = $ ⬜

He spent $ ⬜ altogether.

12. A man buys 5 boxes of oranges. If each box contains 148 oranges, how many oranges will he get?

13. A baker sold 1,380 cakes last month. He sold 3 times as many cakes this month as last month. How many cakes did he sell this month?

14. The total cost of a scooter and 2 motorcycles is $9,798. The cost of each motorcycle is $3,654. Find the cost of the scooter.

15. Maysie had $1,000 to spend. She bought 3 side-tables at $102 each. She also bought a couch for $345. How much money did she have left over?

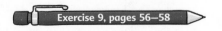

Exercise 9, pages 56—58

3 Division by Ones and Tens

Monty puts 723 stamps equally into 3 packets.
How many stamps are there in each packet?

$723 \div 3 = 241$

There are 241 stamps in each packet.

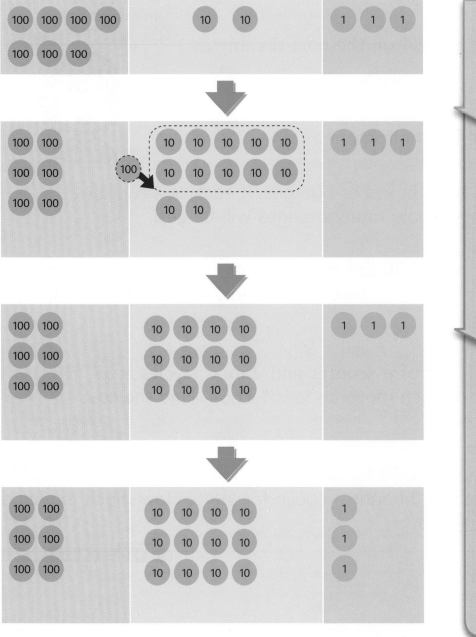

Divide the hundreds by 3.

```
      2
  3 ) 7 2 3
      6
      1
```

Divide the tens by 3.

```
      2 4
  3 ) 7 2 3
      6
      1 2
      1 2
          0
```

Divide the ones by 3.

```
      2 4 1
  3 ) 7 2 3
      6
      1 2
      1 2
          0
          3
          3
          0
```

1. Divide 268 by 3.

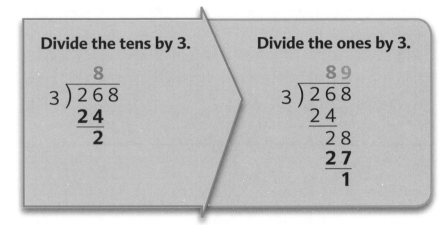

Divide the tens by 3.	Divide the ones by 3.

```
      8
  3 )2 6 8
    2 4
      2
```

```
      8 9
  3 )2 6 8
    2 4
      2 8
      2 7
        1
```

Check: (89 × 3) + 1 = ⬜

2. Divide 692 by 4.

Here is another way to show division.

692 ÷ 4 = ⬜

	4	692
4 x ? = 600 100	4 0 0	−4 0 0
		2 9 2
4 x ? = 292 70	2 8 0	−2 8 0
		1 2
4 x ? = 12 + 3	1 2	−1 2
173	6 9 2	0

692 ÷ 4 = 173

3. Divide 835 by 3.

$835 \div 3 = \boxed{}$

		3	835
$3 \times ? = 800$	200	600	$-\ 600$
			235
$3 \times ? = 235$	70	210	$-\ 210$
			25
$3 \times ? = 25$	$+\ \ \ 8$	24	$-\ \ \ 24$
	278	834	1

$835 \div 3 = 278$ R 1
$(3 \times 278) + 1 = 835$

4. Divide.
   (a) $70 \div 3$ (b) $65 \div 4$ (c) $95 \div 5$
   (d) $500 \div 3$ (e) $805 \div 4$ (f) $850 \div 5$
   (g) $216 \div 6$ (h) $504 \div 7$ (i) $482 \div 8$

5. Estimate the value of $438 \div 7$.

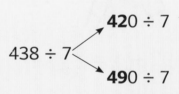

438 ÷ 7
→ 420 ÷ 7
→ 490 ÷ 7

438 is nearer to 420 than 490.

$438 \div 7 = \boxed{}$

The value of $438 \div 7$ is about $\boxed{}$.

6. Estimate and then divide.
   (a) $693 \div 7$ (b) $474 \div 6$ (c) $736 \div 8$
   (d) $576 \div 4$ (e) $678 \div 6$ (f) $935 \div 5$

Exercise 10, pages 59–60

7. Divide 8,492 by 6.

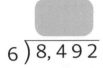

6) 8, 4 9 2

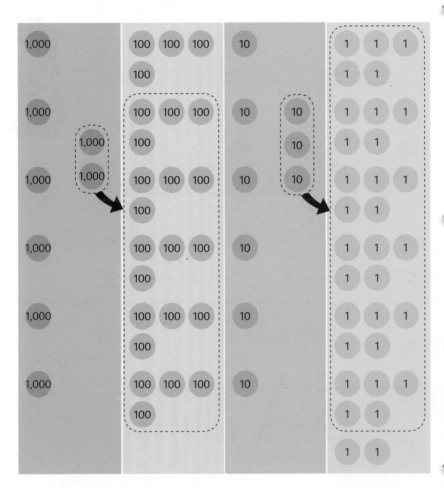

Check the answer. Does
(1,415 × 6) + 2 = 8,492?

Divide the thousands by 6.

```
     1,
6 ) 8, 4 9 2
     6
     2
```

Divide the hundreds by 6.

```
     1, 4
6 ) 8, 4 9 2
     6
     2 4
     2 4
       0
```

Divide the tens by 6.

```
     1, 4 1
6 ) 8, 4 9 2
     6
     2 4
     2 4
       0 9
         6
         3
```

Divide the ones by 6.

```
     1, 4 1 5
6 ) 8, 4 9 2
     6
     2 4
     2 4
       0 9
         6
         3 2
         3 0
           2
```

8. Maurice earned $4,540 in 5 months. He earned the same amount in each of the 5 months. How much did he earn in the first month?

Divide 4,540 by 5.

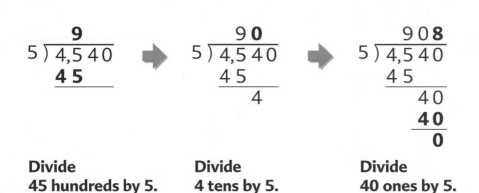

| Divide 45 hundreds by 5. | Divide 4 tens by 5. | Divide 40 ones by 5. |

9. Divide 4,207 by 3.

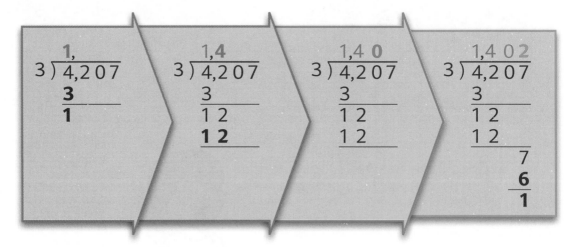

We can also show our work this way.

$3 \times ? = 4{,}000$ $1{,}000$

$3 \times ? = 1{,}207$ 400

$3 \times ? = 7$ $+ \quad 2$

$1{,}402$

		3
	3,000
	1,200
	6
	4,206

```
      4, 2 0 7
   -  3, 0 0 0
      1, 2 0 7
   -  1, 2 0 0
            7
   -        6
            1
```

$4{,}207 \div 3 =$ R ⬜

$(3 \times$ ⬜ $) +$ ⬜ $= 4{,}207$

10. Estimate the value of $3{,}840 \div 6$.

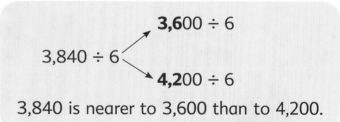

$3{,}840 \div 6$ ⟶ $\mathbf{3{,}6}00 \div 6$

⟶ $\mathbf{4{,}2}00 \div 6$

3,840 is nearer to 3,600 than to 4,200.

$3{,}600 \div 6 =$ ⬜

The value of $3{,}840 \div 6$ is about ⬜.

11. (a) Estimate the value of 7,982 ÷ 7.

$$7,000 \div 7 = 1,000 \qquad 7,700 \div 7 = 1,100$$

(b) Find the value of 7,982 ÷ 7.

```
7 ) 7,9 8 2
```

```
      1
7 ) 7,9 8 2
    7
    0
```
→
```
      1 1
7 ) 7,9 8 2
    7
    0 9
      7
      2
```
→
```
      1 1 4
7 ) 7,9 8 2
    7
    0 9
      7
      2 8
      2 8
        0
```
→
```
      1 1 4 0
7 ) 7,9 8 2
    7
    0 9
      7
      2 8
      2 8
        0 2
```

When 7,982 is divided by 7, the quotient is ⬚

and the remainder is ⬚ .

12. Find the value of each of the following.

(a) 40 ÷ 10 = ⬚

(b) 400 ÷ 10 = ⬚

   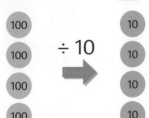

(c) $440 \div 10 = $ ☐

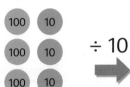

What pattern do you observe?

(d) $4,440 \div 10 = $ ☐

13. Divide 3,245 by 10.

$$
\begin{array}{r}
3 \\
10\overline{)3,2\,4\,5} \\
3\,0 \\
\hline
2
\end{array}
\qquad
\begin{array}{r}
3\,2 \\
10\overline{)3,2\,4\,5} \\
3\,0 \\
\hline
2\,4 \\
2\,0 \\
\hline
4
\end{array}
\qquad
\begin{array}{r}
3\,2\,4 \\
10\overline{)3,2\,4\,5} \\
3\,0 \\
\hline
2\,4 \\
2\,0 \\
\hline
4\,5 \\
4\,0 \\
\hline
5
\end{array}
$$

$3,245 \div 10 = $ ☐ $\div 10 + $ ☐

14. Estimate and then divide.

(a) $3,604 \div 9$ (b) $3,580 \div 7$ (c) $3,120 \div 8$

(d) $8,128 \div 10$ (e) $7,528 \div 3$ (f) $7,180 \div 6$

(g) $9,347 \div 5$ (h) $8,500 \div 10$ (i) $2,948 \div 10$

15. Replace the letters with a number to make the equation true.

   (a) $n \times 10 = 4{,}520$
   (b) $8 \times n = 3{,}944$
   (c) $m \div 6 = 1{,}432$
   (d) $m \div 5 = 6{,}905$

Exercise 11, pages 61–63

16. The number of cars is 4 times the number of motorcycles in a town.

   There are more cars than motorcycles.

   (a) If there are 4,356 cars, how many motorcycles are there?

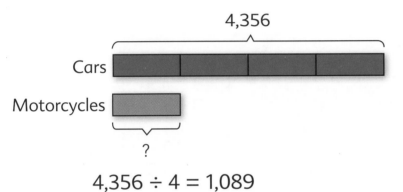

4,356

Cars

Motorcycles

?

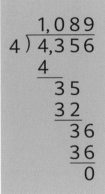

$$\begin{array}{r} 1{,}089 \\ 4\overline{)4{,}356} \\ 4\phantom{{,}356} \\ \hline 35 \\ 32 \\ \hline 36 \\ 36 \\ \hline 0 \end{array}$$

$4{,}356 \div 4 = 1{,}089$

There are 1,089 motorcycles.

   (b) How many cars and motorcycles are there altogether?

   Method 1:
   $4{,}356 + 1{,}089 = \boxed{}$

   There are $\boxed{}$ cars and motorcycles altogether.

   Method 2:
   $1{,}089 \times 5 = \boxed{}$

   There are $\boxed{}$ cars and motorcycles altogether.

17. At one wing of a stadium, the seats are divided into 5 sections. Each section has 1,825 seats. How many seats are there in the wing?

1,825

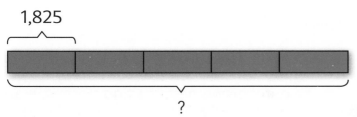

?

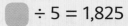
$\boxed{} \div 5 = 1,825$
We multiply to find the missing number.

$\boxed{} \div 5 = 1,825$

$1,825 \times 5 = \boxed{}$

There are $\boxed{}$ seats in the wing.

1,825 is approximately 2,000.
$2,000 \times 5 = 10,000$
Is your answer reasonable?

18. Susan saved $9,600 in 5 months. If she saved an equal amount of money each month, how much will she save in 8 months?

$\boxed{} \times 5 = 9,600$

$9,600 \div 5 = \boxed{}$

$9,600 \rightarrow 10,000$
$10,000 \div 5 = 2,000$
$2,000 \times 8 = 16,000$
Is the answer close to 16,000?

She saved $\$\boxed{}$ each month.

$\boxed{} \times 8 = \boxed{}$

She will save $\$\boxed{}$ in 8 months.

19. Ms. Woods withdrew a sum of money from her bank account. She spent $1,140 of the money on a laptop computer and donated the rest to 3 charities. Each charity received $1,060 from Ms. Woods. How much money did she withdraw?

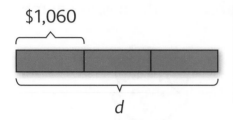

$1,060

d

We can use a letter to represent the number we need to find. Here, we use *d* to represent the total amount of money Ms. Woods donated.
$d \div 3 = \$1,060$

$d \div 3 = 1,060$

$d = 1,060 \times 3 = $ ⬜

She donated $ ⬜ .

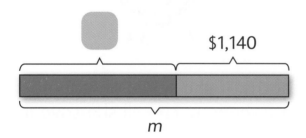

⬜

$1,140

m

We can use *m* to represent the amount of money Ms. Woods withdrew.

$m = $ ⬜ $ + 1,140$

$= $ ⬜

She withdrew $ ⬜ .

20. 8,604 liters of sports drink were consumed at a marathon this year. This was three times the amount of sports drink consumed at the marathon last year.

(a) How many liters of sports drink were consumed at the marathon last year?

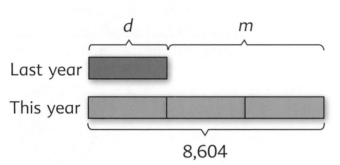

We let *d* be the amount of sports drink consumed last year. We can let *m* be the difference in the amount consumed between this year and last year.

$d \times 3 = 8{,}604$

$d = 8{,}604 \div 3$

$ = $

 liters of sports drink were consumed last year.

(b) How much more sports drink was consumed this year than last year?

Method 1:

$m = 8{,}604 - $

$ = $

Method 2:

$d \times 2 = \times 2$

$ = $

Estimate.
(a) $9{,}000 \div 3 = 3{,}000$
(b) $9{,}000 - 3{,}000 = 6{,}000$
    or
    $3{,}000 \times 2 = 6{,}000$
Are your answers reasonable?

more liters of sports drink were consumed this year.

21. A school wants to know how many loaves of bread it needs to order for 390 students such that each student will have 3 meals with 1 serving of bread. About 5 servings can be made from 1 loaf of bread. About how many loaves of bread should be ordered?

The school just needs an estimated number of servings. So, round 390 to the nearest hundred.

Number of servings = 400 × 3
= 1,200

We need a more exact answer at this step so that we will not order too many loaves of bread!

Number of loaves of bread = 1,200 ÷ 5

=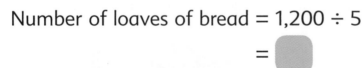

About ⬜ loaves of bread should be ordered.

22. A bakery is boxing up 5,924 loaves of bread to deliver to some supermarkets. Each box can hold 8 loaves. How many boxes are needed?

The bakery needs ⬜ full boxes and ⬜ partially full box.

23. 3,500 spectators were at a football game. There were 4 times as many men as women. How many women were at the football game?

24. The cost of a computer is 4 times the cost of a printer. If the computer costs $2,560, find the cost of the printer.

25. Josh had 1,536 rubber bands. He put them equally into 6 boxes. How many rubber bands were there in each box?

26. James bought 3,757 kg of potatoes. He wants to pack the potatoes into bags that can hold 10 kg each at most. What is the smallest number of bags that he needs?

27. For the last four months, Jake earned a fixed sum of money monthly. During this period, he spent $3,032 and saved the remaining $4,548. How much did Jake earn each month?

28. Mrs. Tilly started reading a 6,958-page book. If she only has time to read 10 pages per day, what is the least number of days she needs to complete the book?

Exercise 12, pages 64–65

4 Multiplication by a 2-Digit Number

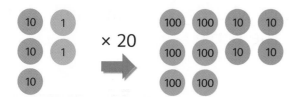

32 × 10 = 320   320 × 2 = 640

32 × 2 = 64   64 × 10 = 640

32 × 20 = 640

1. Multiply.

    (a) 16 × 10   (b) 40 × 10   (c) 254 × 10
    (d) 10 × 29   (e) 10 × 96   (f) 10 × 380

2. Find the product of 14 and 30.

Method 1:
$14 \times 30 = 14 \times 10 \times 3$
$= 140 \times 3$
$=$

Method 2:
$14 \times 30 = 14 \times 3 \times 10$
$= 42 \times 10$
$=$

Method 3:
$14 \times 3 = 42$
$14 \times 3\mathbf{0} = 42\mathbf{0}$

3. Multiply.

(a) $284 \times 20 =$

(b) $40 \times 309 =$

```
        2 8 4
    ×     2 0
    ─────────
      5, 6 8 0
```

```
        3 0 9
    ×     4 0
    ─────────
    1 2, 3 6 0
```

4. Multiply.

(a) 23×30 (b) 68×70 (c) 392×80
(d) 50×36 (e) 90×45 (f) 560×60

Exercise 13, page 66

73

5. Mr. Li bought 12 boxes of mangoes. There were 18 mangoes in each box. How many mangoes did he buy altogether?

$18 \times 10 = 180$ $18 \times 2 = 36$

$18 \times 12 = 180 + 36 = \boxed{}$

He bought ⬜ mangoes altogether.

	1 8
×	1 2
	3 6

Multiply 18 by 2.

	1 8
×	1 2
	3 6
	1 8 0

Multiply 18 by 10.

	1 8
×	1 2
	3 6
	1 8 0
	2 1 6

Add the products.

6. Multiply 34 by 15.

$34 \times 15 =$ ⬜

$34 \times 5 = 170$
$34 \times 10 = 340$
$34 \times 15 = 340 + 170$

Method 1:

```
    3 4              3 4              3 4
×   1 5          ×   1 5          ×   1 5
─────────        ─────────        ─────────
  1 7 0            1 7 0            1 7 0
                   3 4 0            3 4 0
                                 ─────────
                                   5 1 0
```

Method 2:

	30	4
10	$30 \times 10 = 300$	$4 \times 10 = 40$
5	$30 \times 5 = 150$	$4 \times 5 = 20$

```
    3 0 0
    1 5 0
        4 0
+       2 0
─────────────
    ⬜
─────────────
```

7. Multiply.

$64 \times 27 =$ ⬜

Method 1:

```
      6 4
×     2 7
─────────────
      4 4 8   ←——— 64 × 7
  1, 2 8 0   ←——— 64 × 20
─────────────
  1, 7 2 8
```

Method 2:

	60	4
20	60 × 20 = 1,200	4 × 20 = 80
7	60 × 7 = 420	4 × 7 = 28

```
  1,2 0 0
    4 2 0
       8 0
+     2 8
_____
```

8. Multiply.

   (a) 29 × 48
   (d) 56 × 69

   (b) 36 × 27
   (e) 18 × 78

   (c) 29 × 92
   (f) 52 × 19

Exercise 14, page 67

9. Find the product of 53 and 847.

   Method 1:

```
        8 4 7
   ×      5 3
   _____
      2, 5 4 1   ←——— 847 × 3
   4 2, 3 5 0   ←——— 847 × 50 = 847 × 5 × 10
   _____
```

847 × 53 = (× 50) + (847 ×   ) =

76

Method 2:

	800	40	7
50	800 × 50 = 40,000	40 × 50 = 2,000	7 × 50 = 350
3	800 × 3 = 2,400	40 × 3 = 120	7 × 3 = 21

```
  4 0,0 0 0
    2,4 0 0
    2,0 0 0
      1 2 0
      3 5 0
+       2 1
  _____
```
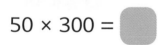

10. Multiply.

    (a) 20 × 60   (b) 50 × 80   (c) 70 × 90
    (d) 500 × 30   (e) 40 × 600   (f) 400 × 50

11. Estimate the value of 32 × 68.

$$30 \times 70 = \boxed{}$$

The value of 32 × 68 is about $\boxed{}$.

12. Estimate the value of 48 × 315.

$$50 \times 300 = \boxed{}$$

The value of 48 × 315 is about $\boxed{}$.

13. Estimate and then multiply.

    (a) 49 × 18   (b) 21 × 72   (c) 62 × 47
    (d) 412 × 23   (e) 383 × 58   (f) 685 × 32
    (g) 51 × 490   (h) 69 × 786   (i) 88 × 594

Exercise 15, pages 68–70

14. (a) $19 \times 278 =$

Method 1:

```
      2  7  8
 ×       1  9
 ─────────────
   2, 5 0 2  ←──── 278 × 9
   2, 7 8 0  ←──── 278 × 10
 ─────────────
   5, 2 8 2
```

Method 2:

$19 \times 278 = 20 \times 278 - 278$

$20 \times 278 = 5{,}560$
$19 \times 278 = 5{,}560 - 278 = 5{,}282$

(b) $36 \times 99 =$

$36 \times 99 = 36 \times 100 - 36$

$36 \times 100 = 3{,}600$
$36 \times 99 = 3{,}600 - 36$
$=$

(c) $28 \times 25 =$

$4 \times 25 = 100$

$\mathbf{28} \times 25 = \mathbf{7} \times \mathbf{4} \times 25$
$= 7 \times 100$
$=$

15. Multiply.

   (a) 8 × 99   (b) 24 × 99   (c) 36 × 99
   (d) 99 × 9   (e) 99 × 47   (f) 99 × 38
   (g) 8 × 25   (h) 36 × 25   (i) 44 × 25
   (j) 25 × 12   (k) 25 × 52   (l) 25 × 72

16. Miguel delivers 165 copies of a newspaper every day. How many copies of the newspaper will he deliver in 30 days?

17. Tom bought 15 sheets of stamps. If there were 25 stamps on each sheet, how many stamps did he buy?

18. After buying 12 chairs at $128 each, Catherine had $342 left. How much money did she have at first?

19. Each school bus can carry a maximum of 40 students. There were 15 such buses for an excursion. How many students were there altogether if all the buses were filled?

20. Mr. Han earns $30,000 in a year. If he spends $925 each month over 12 months and saves the rest, how much can he save in a year?

21. Mrs. Garcia saved $2,001 in two years. She saved $65 a month in the first 15 months. She saved the same amount every month in the next 9 months. How much did she save a month in the next 9 months?

Exercise 16, pages 71–73

1. Which of the following expressions does **not** have the same value as 1,998 + 998?

   (A) 1,998 + 1,000 − 2
   (B) 998 + 2,000 − 2
   (C) 2,000 + 1,000 − 2
   (D) 2,000 + 1,000 − 4

2. Find the value of 2,590 + 109 − 484.

   (A) 2,106
   (B) 2,215
   (C) 2,699
   (D) 2,965

3. Which of the following expressions has the same value as 318 × 9?

   (A) (800 × 9) + (10 × 9) + (3 × 9)
   (B) (300 × 9) + (10 × 9) + (8 × 9)
   (C) (300 × 9) + (80 × 9) + (1 × 9)
   (D) (100 × 9) + (30 × 9) + (8 × 9)

4. What is the remainder of 234 ÷ 8?

   (A) 1   (B) 2
   (C) 3   (D) 4

5. What is the product of 643 and 7?

600	40	7
7 | 600 × 7 =	40 × 7 =	7 × 7 =

   (A) 4,200
   (B) 4,480
   (C) 4,501
   (D) 4,529

6. Select True or False for the following.
   (a) $458 + 992 = 458 + 1,000 - 8$ True / False
   (b) $6,521 - 702 = 6,521 - 700 + 2$ True / False

7. Select True or False for the following.
   (a) $399 \times 60 = 399 \times 6 \times 10$ True / False
   (b) $m \div 5 = 6,905$
       So, $m = 6,905 \div 5$ True / False

8. Estimate and then find the value of each of the following.
   (a) Find the sum of 4,786 and 599.
   (b) Find the difference between 2,976 and 5,076.
   (c) Find the product of 6 and 306.
   (d) Find the quotient and remainder when 3,650 is divided by 8.

9. What is the value of n in each of the following?
   (a) $n \times 8 = 2,896$ (b) $n \div 7 = 715$
   (c) $36 \times 25 = 9 \times n$ (d) $n \div 10 = 7,102$

10. Find the product of the following.
    (a) 210×30 (b) 456×60 (c) 905×80

11. Estimate and then multiply.
    (a) 39×19 (b) 48×25 (c) 99×4
    (d) 208×31 (e) 512×28 (f) 198×6
    (g) 295×49 (h) 66×582 (i) $5,837 \times 4$

12. Find the value of each of the following expressions.
    (a) $(26 + 18) \times 12$ (b) $23 \times (83 - 43)$
    (c) $(635 - 30) \div 5$ (d) $6,408 \div (48 - 45)$

13. The product of two numbers is 888. If one of the numbers is 6, what is the other number?

14. A blue ribbon is 1,242 cm long. A red ribbon is 9 times as long as the blue ribbon. How long is the red ribbon?

15. A shopkeeper packed 3,284 cakes of soap into 8 equal packages.
    (a) How many cakes of soap were there in each package?
    (b) How many cakes of soap were left over?

16. Susan saved $370 in 5 weeks. If she saved an equal amount each week, how much would she save in 8 weeks?

17. Twelve pieces of ribbon, each 75 in. long, are cut from a length of ribbon 1,250 in. long. What is the length of the remaining piece of ribbon?

18. Robert bought a washing machine and 3 microwave ovens for $2,000. The washing machine cost $665. How much did each microwave oven cost?

19. A teacher and 18 students went to an aquarium. The total entrance fee was $233. The entrance fee for each student was $11. What was the entrance fee for the teacher?

20. The cost of renting a truck is $4,500 a month. 4 men rented a truck for 2 months. They shared the cost equally. How much did each man pay?

21. 3,000 exercise books are arranged in 3 piles. The first pile has 10 more books than the second pile. The number of books in the second pile is twice the number of books in the third pile. How many books are there in the third pile?

22. The sum of four numbers, *A*, *B*, *C* and *D*, is 1,000. *B* is 140 less than *A*. *C* is 20 more than *A* and 20 more than *D*. What number is *A*?

23. 45 people took part in a swimming competition. The number of people who took part in a walkathon was 12 times the number of people who took part in the swimming competition. How many more people took part in the walkathon than in the swimming competition?

24. Rolando ordered 138 boxes of mangoes. There were 24 mangoes in each box. He kept 72 mangoes and sold the rest to 3 customers. If each customer bought an equal number of mangoes, how many mangoes did each customer buy?

25. Show two ways to find the product of 309 and 14.

26. Show two ways to find the value of 956 ÷ 4.

27. Find the quotient and remainder of 1,372 ÷ 6. How can you use multiplication to check whether your answer is correct? Explain your answer.

Review 2, pages 74–80

3 FRACTIONS

1 Equivalent Fractions

Mandy, Serena and Alex each bought a pizza of the same size.

I cut the pizza into 3 equal parts and ate 1 part.
I ate $\frac{1}{3}$ of the pizza.

I cut the pizza into 6 equal parts and ate 2 parts.
I ate $\frac{2}{6}$ of the pizza.

I cut the pizza into 9 equal parts and ate 3 parts.
I ate $\frac{3}{9}$ of the pizza.

$$\frac{1}{3} = \frac{2}{6} = \frac{3}{9}$$

$\frac{1}{3}$, $\frac{2}{6}$ and $\frac{3}{9}$ are **equivalent fractions**.

$\frac{1}{3}$ **is a fraction in its simplest form.**

1. What are the missing numerators and denominators?

(a)

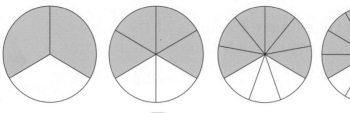

$$\frac{2}{3} = \frac{\boxed{}}{6} = \frac{6}{\boxed{}} = \frac{\boxed{}}{\boxed{}}$$

(b)

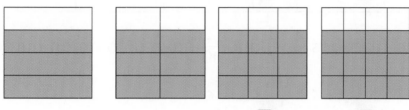

$$\frac{3}{4} = \frac{6}{\boxed{}} = \frac{\boxed{}}{12} = \frac{\boxed{}}{\boxed{}}$$

2. What are the missing numerators and denominators?

(a) $\frac{4}{5} \overset{\times 2}{\underset{\times 2}{=}} \frac{\boxed{}}{10}$

(b) $\frac{1}{4} \overset{\times 3}{\underset{\times 3}{=}} \frac{3}{\boxed{}}$

(c) $\frac{1}{6} = \frac{\boxed{}}{24}$

(d) $\frac{2}{3} = \frac{10}{\boxed{}}$

3. What are the missing numerators and denominators?

(a) $\frac{8}{12} \overset{\div 2}{\underset{\div 2}{=}} \frac{\boxed{}}{6}$

(b) $\frac{9}{15} \overset{\div 3}{\underset{\div 3}{=}} \frac{3}{\boxed{}}$

(c) $\frac{12}{16} = \frac{\boxed{}}{4}$

(d) $\frac{5}{20} = \frac{1}{\boxed{}}$

4. Express each of the following fractions in its simplest form.

(a) $\frac{9}{18}$ (b) $\frac{12}{18}$ (c) $\frac{10}{12}$ (d) $\frac{16}{20}$

Exercise 1, pages 81–84

5. Arrange the fractions in order.

(a)

It is easy to compare fractions of the same whole when they have a common numerator or a common denominator.

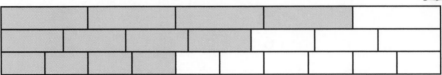

The fractions $\frac{4}{5}$, $\frac{4}{7}$ and $\frac{4}{10}$ have a common numerator.

$\square < \square < \square$

(b)

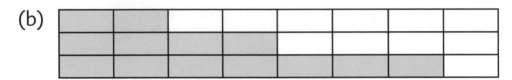

The fractions $\frac{2}{8}$, $\frac{4}{8}$ and $\frac{7}{8}$ have a common denominator.

$\square < \square < \square$

6. (a) Which is greater, $\frac{2}{3}$ or $\frac{5}{6}$?

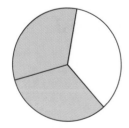

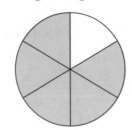

$\frac{2}{3} = \frac{\square}{6}$

(b) Which is greater, $\frac{4}{5}$ or $\frac{7}{10}$?

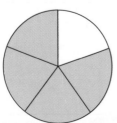

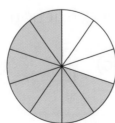

$\frac{4}{5} = \frac{\square}{10}$

7. Arrange the fractions in increasing order.

(a) $\frac{3}{5}$, $\frac{1}{2}$, $\frac{9}{10}$

10 is a common multiple of 2, 5 and 10.

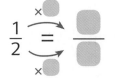 $\frac{1}{2} = \frac{5}{10}$ ×5 $\frac{3}{5} = \frac{6}{10}$ ×2

In increasing order: $\frac{1}{2}$, $\frac{3}{5}$, $\frac{9}{10}$

(b) $\frac{1}{2}$, $\frac{3}{4}$, $\frac{2}{3}$

 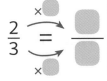

In increasing order:

(a) $\frac{5}{10}$ $\frac{6}{10}$ $\frac{9}{10}$

↓

$\frac{1}{2}$ $\frac{3}{5}$ $\frac{9}{10}$

(b) 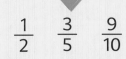 is a common multiple of 2, 3 and 4.

8. (a) Is $\frac{5}{8}$ greater than or smaller than $\frac{1}{2}$?

When comparing a fraction to $\frac{1}{2}$, multiply its numerator by 2. If the product is greater than the fraction's denominator, the fraction is greater than $\frac{1}{2}$.

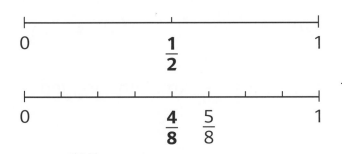

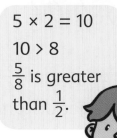

5 × 2 = 10
10 > 8
$\frac{5}{8}$ is greater than $\frac{1}{2}$.

87

(b) Is $\frac{2}{5}$ greater than or smaller than $\frac{1}{2}$?

Is 5 > 2 × 2?

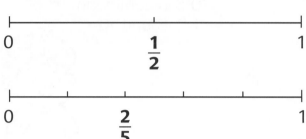

(c) Which is greater, $\frac{2}{5}$ or $\frac{5}{8}$?

9. Which of the following fractions are greater than $\frac{1}{2}$?

(a) $\frac{2}{5}$ (b) $\frac{4}{6}$ (c) $\frac{7}{12}$ (d) $\frac{5}{9}$

10. (a) Which is smaller, $\frac{5}{6}$ or $\frac{4}{5}$?

$\frac{5}{6}$ is $\frac{1}{6}$ from 1.

$\frac{4}{5}$ is $\frac{1}{5}$ from 1.

$\frac{1}{6} < \frac{1}{5}$

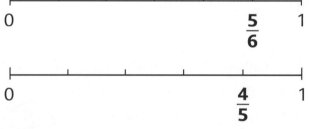

(b) Which is greater, $\frac{11}{12}$ or $\frac{9}{10}$?

11. Arrange the fractions in increasing order.

(a) $\frac{7}{12}, \frac{3}{4}, \frac{2}{3}$ (b) $\frac{3}{4}, \frac{6}{7}, \frac{1}{2}$ (c) $\frac{2}{5}, \frac{5}{7}, \frac{5}{8}$

12. Brian jogged $\frac{3}{4}$ km. Erin jogged $\frac{7}{10}$ km. Who jogged a longer distance?

Exercise 2, pages 85–86

88

② Adding and Subtracting Like Fractions

5 wholes = 1 whole + 2 wholes + 2 wholes

5 = 1 + 2 + 2

5 eighths = 1 eighth + 2 eighths + 2 eighths

$\frac{5}{8} = \frac{1}{8} + \frac{2}{8} + \frac{2}{8}$

(a) Find different ways to make 5.

$5 = 1 + 1 + 1 + 1 + 1$
$5 = 1 + 4$
$5 = 1 + 1 + 3$
...

(b) Find different ways to make $\frac{5}{8}$ using eighths.

(c) Find different ways to make $\frac{5}{9}$ using ninths.

1. Find different ways to make $\frac{7}{9}$ using ninths.

2. Find different ways to make 1 whole using fourths.

3. What are the missing numerators?

(a) $\frac{\boxed{}}{8} = \frac{1}{8} + \frac{2}{8} + \frac{3}{8}$

(b) $\frac{1}{4} + \frac{\boxed{}}{4} = \frac{1}{4} + \frac{1}{4} + \frac{1}{4} + \frac{1}{4}$

(c) $1 = \frac{1}{7} + \frac{2}{7} + \frac{\boxed{}}{7}$

(d) $\frac{1}{10} + \frac{3}{10} + \frac{5}{10} = \frac{4}{10} + \frac{\boxed{}}{10} + \frac{3}{10}$

4. Lila drank $\frac{1}{5}$ of a liter of milk.

    Her brother drank $\frac{2}{5}$ of a liter of milk.

    How much milk did they drink altogether?

  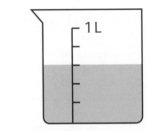

$\frac{1}{5} + \frac{2}{5} = \boxed{}$

1 fifth + 2 fifths = 3 fifths

They drank $\boxed{}$ liters of milk altogether.

5. Find the sum of $\frac{2}{5}$ and $\frac{3}{5}$.

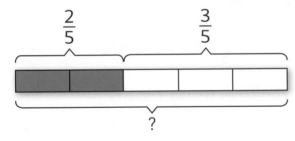

$\frac{2}{5} + \frac{3}{5} = \boxed{}$

2 fifths + 3 fifths = 1 whole

6. (a) Add $\frac{3}{8}$ and $\frac{2}{8}$.

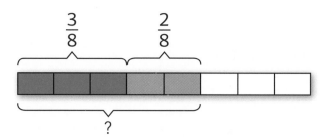

$$\frac{3}{8} + \frac{2}{8} = \frac{\boxed{}}{8}$$

(b) Add $\frac{5}{8}$ and $\frac{1}{8}$.

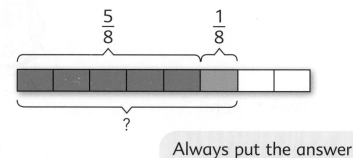

$$\frac{5}{8} + \frac{1}{8} = \frac{\boxed{}}{8}$$

$$= \boxed{}$$

Always put the answer in the simplest form.

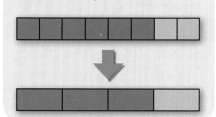

7. Add.

(a) $\frac{1}{9} + \frac{4}{9}$

(b) $\frac{2}{7} + \frac{2}{7}$

(c) $\frac{4}{6} + \frac{1}{6}$

(d) $\frac{1}{6} + \frac{3}{6}$

(e) $\frac{1}{4} + \frac{3}{4}$

(f) $\frac{3}{10} + \frac{5}{10}$

(g) $\frac{3}{7} + \frac{4}{7}$

(h) $\frac{2}{9} + \frac{4}{9}$

(i) $\frac{5}{12} + \frac{1}{12}$

(j) $\frac{2}{5} + \frac{2}{5} + \frac{1}{5}$

(k) $\frac{3}{7} + \frac{3}{7} + \frac{1}{7}$

(l) $\frac{2}{9} + \frac{2}{9} + \frac{2}{9}$

Exercise 3, pages 87–90

8. Debbie had $\frac{7}{8}$ of a pie.

   She ate $\frac{2}{8}$ of the pie.

   What fraction of the pie was left?

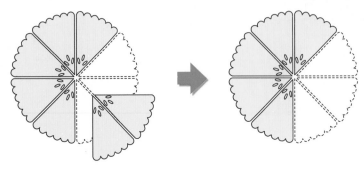

$$\frac{7}{8} - \frac{2}{8} = \boxed{}$$

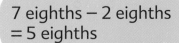

$\boxed{}$ of the pie was left.

7 eighths − 2 eighths
= 5 eighths

9. Find the difference between $\frac{4}{5}$ and $\frac{3}{5}$.

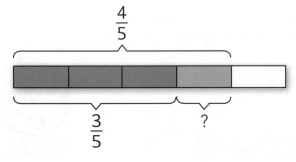

$$\frac{4}{5} - \frac{3}{5} = \boxed{}$$

4 fifths − 3 fifths
= 1 fifth

10. Subtract $\frac{3}{10}$ from 1.

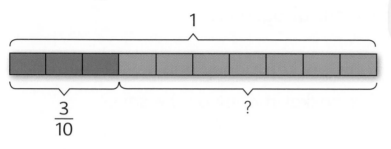

$1 = \frac{10}{10}$

$1 - \frac{3}{10} = \boxed{}$

11. Subtract $\frac{1}{8}$ from $\frac{5}{8}$.

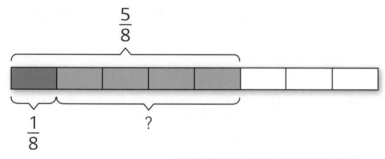

$\frac{5}{8} - \frac{1}{8} = \dfrac{\boxed{}}{8}$

$= \boxed{}$

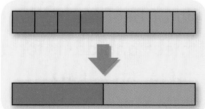

12. Subtract.

(a) $\frac{4}{5} - \frac{1}{5}$

(b) $\frac{6}{8} - \frac{5}{8}$

(c) $\frac{7}{9} - \frac{3}{9}$

(d) $\frac{3}{4} - \frac{1}{4}$

(e) $\frac{7}{10} - \frac{3}{10}$

(f) $\frac{8}{12} - \frac{5}{12}$

(g) $1 - \frac{2}{9}$

(h) $1 - \frac{9}{10}$

(i) $1 - \frac{7}{12}$

(j) $1 - \frac{2}{5} - \frac{2}{5}$

(k) $\frac{7}{8} - \frac{1}{8} - \frac{3}{8}$

(l) $\frac{8}{9} - \frac{1}{9} - \frac{4}{9}$

13. Sally ate $\frac{1}{8}$ of a cake and her sister ate $\frac{3}{8}$ of it. What fraction of the cake did they eat altogether?

14. Marlon spent $\frac{4}{9}$ of his pocket money and saved the rest. What fraction of his pocket money did he save?

15. Fatimah spent $\frac{3}{7}$ of her money on a book. She spent the rest of her money on a racket. What fraction of her money was spent on the racket?

16. Mike baked a pie. He ate $\frac{1}{6}$ of the pie and gave $\frac{3}{6}$ of the pie to his friends. What fraction of the pie did he have left?

17. Chris spent $\frac{5}{12}$ of his savings on a laptop. He spent $\frac{3}{12}$ of his savings on a printer. What fraction of his savings did he spend altogether?

18. Mr. Kim bought $\frac{3}{10}$ kg of beef and $\frac{6}{10}$ kg of chicken. He cooked $\frac{2}{10}$ kg of meat and ate it for dinner. How many kilograms of meat did he have left?

19. Irene had $\frac{4}{5}$ m of ribbon. She used $\frac{3}{5}$ m to tie presents. She then bought $\frac{2}{5}$ m more ribbon. How many meters of ribbon did she have in the end?

Exercise 4, pages 91–93

3 Mixed Numbers

This strip of paper is longer than 1 m.

1 m $\frac{1}{2}$ m

It is $1\frac{1}{2}$ m long.

$1 + \frac{1}{2} = 1\frac{1}{2}$

There are $2\frac{1}{2}$ watermelons.

$2 + \frac{1}{2} = 2\frac{1}{2}$

The total amount of water is $3\frac{3}{4}$ liters.

$3 + \frac{3}{4} = 3\frac{3}{4}$

$1\frac{1}{2}$, $2\frac{1}{2}$ and $3\frac{3}{4}$ are **mixed numbers**.

When we add a whole number and a fraction, the result is a mixed number.

1. Write a mixed number for each of the following.

(a)

$1 + \frac{1}{3} = \boxed{}$

1 whole 1 third = $\boxed{}$

(b)

2 wholes 3 fifths = $\boxed{}$

(c)

2 wholes 1 sixth = $\boxed{}$

2. What number does each letter represent?

(a)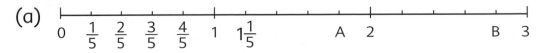

0    $\frac{1}{5}$ $\frac{2}{5}$ $\frac{3}{5}$ $\frac{4}{5}$ 1 $1\frac{1}{5}$ A   2   B   3

(b)

0    $\frac{1}{8}$ $\frac{2}{8}$ $\frac{3}{8}$ $\frac{4}{8}$ $\frac{5}{8}$ $\frac{6}{8}$ $\frac{7}{8}$ 1 $1\frac{1}{8}$ C   D   2

3. Find the value of each of the following.

(a) $3 + \frac{2}{3}$ (b) $\frac{4}{5} + 2$ (c) $\frac{7}{10} + 4$

(d) $2 - \frac{1}{4}$ (e) $3 - \frac{1}{5}$ (f) $5 - \frac{2}{3}$

Exercise 5, pages 94–95

4 Improper Fractions

What is the length of each of the following strips of paper?

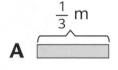

A

$\frac{1}{3}$ m

1 third $= \frac{1}{3}$

B

$\frac{2}{3}$ m

2 thirds $= \frac{2}{3}$

C

$\frac{3}{3}$ m or 1 m

3 thirds $= \frac{3}{3}$

D

$\frac{4}{3}$ m or $1\frac{1}{3}$ m

4 thirds $= \frac{4}{3}$

E

$\frac{5}{3}$ m or $1\frac{2}{3}$ m

5 thirds $= \frac{5}{3}$

$\frac{3}{3}$, $\frac{4}{3}$, and $\frac{5}{3}$ are **improper fractions**.

An improper fraction is equal to or greater than 1.

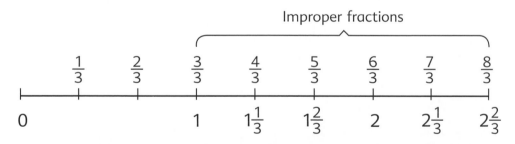

An improper fraction can be expressed
as a whole number or a mixed number.

97

1. How many halves are there in $3\frac{1}{2}$?

$3\frac{1}{2} = \frac{7}{2}$

There are halves in $3\frac{1}{2}$.

2. Write an improper fraction for each of the following.

(a)

$\frac{1}{5} + \frac{1}{5} + \frac{1}{5} + \frac{1}{5} + \frac{1}{5} = \frac{\boxed{}}{5} = \boxed{}$

5 fifths =

(b)

$1 + \frac{1}{4} + \frac{1}{4} + \frac{1}{4}$

$= \frac{4}{4} + \frac{1}{4} + \frac{1}{4} + \frac{1}{4}$

7 quarters =

$= \frac{\boxed{}}{4}$

(c)

$1 + 1$

$= \frac{6}{6} + \frac{6}{6}$

12 sixths =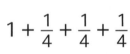

$= \frac{\boxed{}}{6}$

Exercise 6, pages 96—97

3. Change the improper fractions to mixed numbers.

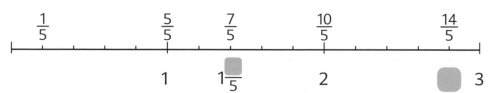

(a) $\dfrac{7}{5} = \dfrac{5}{5} + \dfrac{2}{5}$

$= 1 + \dfrac{2}{5}$

$= 1\dfrac{\boxed{}}{5}$

(b) $\dfrac{14}{5} = \dfrac{10}{5} + \dfrac{4}{5}$

$= 2 + \dfrac{4}{5}$

$= \boxed{}$

4. Change $\dfrac{13}{6}$ to a mixed number.

$\dfrac{13}{6} = \dfrac{12}{6} + \dfrac{1}{6}$

$= 2 + \dfrac{1}{6}$

$= \boxed{}$

$\dfrac{6}{6} = 1$

$\dfrac{12}{6} = 2$

5. Express each of the following as a mixed number or a whole number.

(a) $\dfrac{17}{4}$ (b) $\dfrac{10}{3}$ (c) $\dfrac{8}{2}$ (d) $\dfrac{12}{5}$

Exercise 7, pages 98–99

6. Change the mixed numbers to improper fractions.

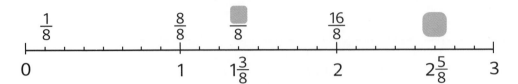

(a) $1\frac{3}{8} = 1 + \frac{3}{8}$

$= \frac{8}{8} + \frac{3}{8}$

$= \frac{\boxed{}}{8}$

(b) $2\frac{5}{8} = 2 + \frac{5}{8}$

$= \frac{16}{8} + \frac{5}{8}$

$= \boxed{}$

7. Change $3\frac{1}{6}$ into an improper fraction.

$3\frac{1}{6} = 3 + \frac{1}{6}$

$= \frac{18}{6} + \frac{1}{6}$

$= \boxed{}$

$1 = \frac{6}{6}$

$3 = \frac{18}{6}$

8. Express each of the following as an improper fraction.

(a) $1\frac{4}{5}$ (b) $2\frac{2}{3}$ (c) $2\frac{1}{4}$ (d) $2\frac{5}{6}$

9. Find the missing numerator in each of the following.

(a) $2\frac{1}{3} = 1\frac{\boxed{}}{3}$

(b) $2\frac{2}{5} = 1\frac{\boxed{}}{5}$

(c) $3\frac{1}{4} = 2\frac{\boxed{}}{4}$

(d) $3\frac{1}{2} = 2\frac{\boxed{}}{2}$

(e) $4\frac{1}{6} = 3\frac{\boxed{}}{6}$

(f) $4\frac{3}{4} = 3\frac{\boxed{}}{4}$

10. Express each of the following as a whole number or a mixed number in its simplest form.

(a) $\frac{10}{4}$

(b) $\frac{12}{3}$

(c) $2\frac{5}{10}$

(d) $2\frac{8}{12}$

(e) $2\frac{8}{5}$

(f) $3\frac{7}{4}$

(g) $1\frac{6}{8}$

(h) $2\frac{6}{3}$

11. Add. Give each answer in its simplest form.

(a) $\frac{5}{6} + \frac{5}{6}$

(b) $\frac{3}{5} + \frac{4}{5}$

(c) $\frac{3}{4} + \frac{1}{4}$

(d) $\frac{6}{7} + \frac{5}{7}$

(e) $\frac{7}{10} + \frac{8}{10}$

(f) $\frac{7}{8} + \frac{6}{8}$

12. Subtract. Give each answer in its simplest form.

(a) $3 - \frac{3}{4}$

(b) $2 - \frac{3}{8}$

(c) $4 - \frac{1}{2}$

(d) $2 - \frac{3}{10}$

(e) $2 - \frac{4}{5}$

(f) $3 - \frac{5}{7}$

Exercise 8, pages 100–104

5 Fractions and Division

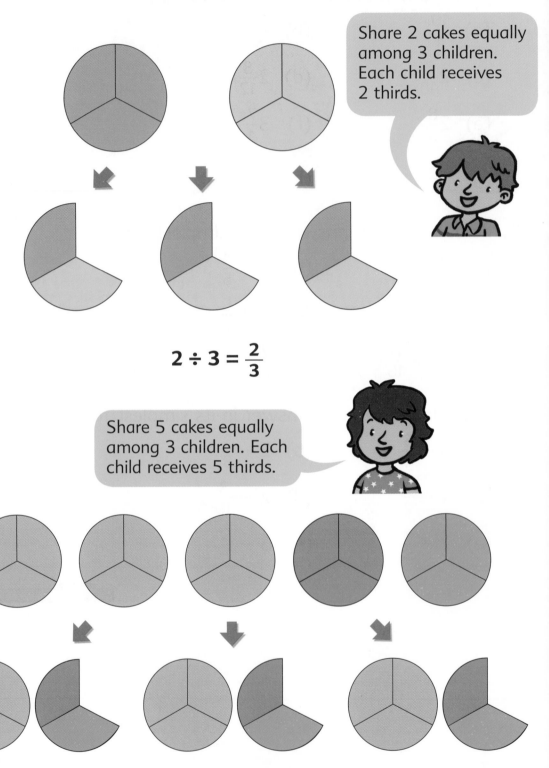

Share 2 cakes equally among 3 children. Each child receives 2 thirds.

$$2 \div 3 = \frac{2}{3}$$

Share 5 cakes equally among 3 children. Each child receives 5 thirds.

$$5 \div 3 = \frac{5}{3}$$

Here is another way to divide 5 by 3.

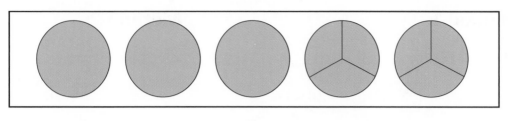

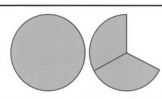 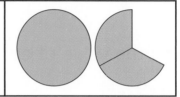

$$5 \div 3 = 1\frac{2}{3}$$

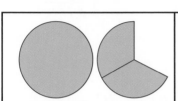

$1\frac{2}{3}$ is the same as $\frac{5}{3}$.

1. A ribbon, 7 m long, is cut into 2 equal pieces.
   What is the length of each piece?

7 m

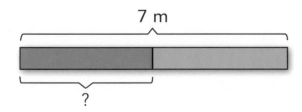

?

$7 \div 2 =$

The length of each piece is ▢ m.

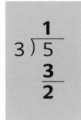

2. Find the value of 26 ÷ 8.

Method 1:

$26 \div 8 = 3\frac{2}{8}$

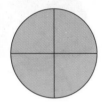

$= 3\frac{\boxed{}}{4}$

$$
\begin{array}{r}
3 \\
8\,\overline{)\,26} \\
24 \\
\hline
2
\end{array}
$$

Method 2:

$26 \div 8 = \frac{26}{8}$

$= \frac{\boxed{}}{4}$

$= \boxed{}$

3. Find the value of each of the following.

   (a) 9 ÷ 4   (b) 13 ÷ 5   (c) 20 ÷ 6

4. Express $\frac{15}{4}$ as a mixed number.

Method 1:

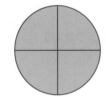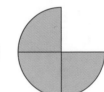

$\frac{15}{4} = \frac{12}{4} + \frac{3}{4}$

$= 3 + \frac{3}{4}$

$= \boxed{}$

Method 2:

$\frac{15}{4} = 15 \div 4 = \boxed{}$

5. A box of apples weighing 3 pounds was divided into 6 equal shares. What was the weight of each share in pounds?

6. Mary cut a ribbon into 4 equal pieces. If the ribbon was 6 m long, how many meters long was each piece?

Exercise 9, pages 105—106

1. Which fraction is not an equivalent fraction of $\frac{4}{6}$?

   (A) $\frac{2}{3}$　　　　(B) $\frac{3}{5}$　　　　(C) $\frac{8}{12}$　　　　(D) $\frac{12}{18}$

2. Which of the following fractions is greater than $\frac{1}{2}$?

   (A) $\frac{2}{5}$　　　　(B) $\frac{4}{7}$　　　　(C) $\frac{4}{10}$　　　　(D) $\frac{5}{12}$

3. What is the fraction represented by P?

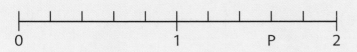

   (A) $\frac{3}{5}$　　　　(B) $1\frac{2}{5}$　　　　(C) $1\frac{3}{5}$　　　　(D) $2\frac{2}{5}$

4. Select True or False for the following.

   (a) $\frac{4}{9} > \frac{1}{2}$ 　　　　　　　　　　　　　　　True / False

   (b) $\frac{5}{6} < \frac{11}{12}$ 　　　　　　　　　　　　　　　True / False

5. Select True or False for the following.

   (a) $1\frac{1}{8} = \frac{11}{8}$ 　　　　　　　　　　　　　　　True / False

   (b) $\frac{2}{7} + \frac{3}{7} + \frac{4}{7} = 1\frac{2}{7}$ 　　　　　　　　　　　True / False

6. Find the missing numerator or denominator.

   (a) $\frac{3}{5} = \frac{\blacksquare}{10}$　　(b) $\frac{1}{6} = \frac{3}{\blacksquare}$　　(c) $\frac{6}{9} = \frac{\blacksquare}{3}$　　(d) $\frac{8}{12} = \frac{2}{\blacksquare}$

7. Name three equivalent fractions for each of these fractions.

   (a) $\frac{2}{3}$ (b) $\frac{1}{5}$ (c) $\frac{9}{12}$

8. What fraction of each figure is shaded?
   Give each answer in its simplest form.

   (a) 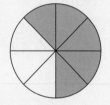   (b) 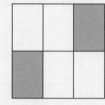   (c)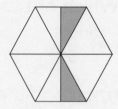

   (d) 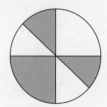   (e)    (f)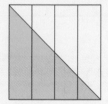

9. Write each fraction in its simplest form.

   (a) $\frac{3}{6}$ (b) $\frac{6}{10}$ (c) $\frac{6}{9}$ (d) $\frac{10}{12}$

   (e) $\frac{10}{15}$ (f) $\frac{18}{24}$ (g) $\frac{20}{40}$ (h) $\frac{12}{60}$

10. Write >, <, or = in place of each ⬤ .

   (a) $\frac{3}{5}$ ⬤ $\frac{1}{2}$ (b) $\frac{3}{7}$ ⬤ $\frac{1}{2}$ (c) $\frac{12}{12}$ ⬤ 1

   (d) $\frac{6}{8}$ ⬤ $\frac{9}{12}$ (e) $\frac{5}{6}$ ⬤ $\frac{7}{9}$ (f) $\frac{3}{4}$ ⬤ $\frac{7}{10}$

11. Arrange the fractions in increasing order.

   (a) $\frac{3}{4}, \frac{2}{3}, \frac{5}{6}$ (b) $\frac{7}{10}, \frac{1}{2}, \frac{2}{5}$

12. $\dfrac{2}{2}$ $\dfrac{5}{8}$ $\dfrac{5}{12}$ $2\dfrac{9}{10}$ $1\dfrac{1}{9}$ $1\dfrac{11}{12}$

    (a) Which of the numbers is nearest to 2?

    (b) Which of them is smaller than $\dfrac{1}{2}$?

Add or subtract. Give each answer in its simplest form.

	(a)	(b)	(c)
13.	$\dfrac{3}{8}+\dfrac{3}{8}$	$\dfrac{2}{5}+\dfrac{1}{5}$	$\dfrac{6}{10}+\dfrac{2}{10}$
14.	$\dfrac{8}{9}-\dfrac{3}{9}$	$\dfrac{5}{6}-\dfrac{2}{6}$	$1-\dfrac{9}{12}$
15.	$\dfrac{1}{9}+\dfrac{4}{9}+\dfrac{2}{9}$	$\dfrac{2}{7}+\dfrac{2}{7}+\dfrac{2}{7}$	$\dfrac{5}{12}+\dfrac{3}{12}+\dfrac{2}{12}$
16.	$\dfrac{7}{8}-\dfrac{1}{8}-\dfrac{3}{8}$	$\dfrac{8}{9}-\dfrac{2}{9}-\dfrac{2}{9}$	$1-\dfrac{3}{7}-\dfrac{2}{7}$

17. Find the number represented by n to make each equation true.

    (a) $\dfrac{4}{7}+n=1$ (b) $\dfrac{7}{9}+n=1$

    (c) $1-\dfrac{3}{10}=n$ (d) $1-n=\dfrac{1}{12}$

18. Find the value of each of the following.

    (a) $4+\dfrac{5}{8}$ (b) $\dfrac{7}{10}+6$ (c) $3-\dfrac{1}{6}$ (d) $5-\dfrac{2}{5}$

19. Write a mixed number or a proper fraction in the simplest form for A, B, C, and D.

20. Write an improper fraction for each of the following.

   (a) 6 sixths   (b) 7 thirds   (c) 12 quarters   (d) 8 fifths

21. Express each of the following as a whole number or a mixed number in its simplest form.

   (a) $\frac{10}{3}$ (b) $\frac{15}{5}$ (c) $\frac{18}{4}$ (d) $\frac{23}{7}$

   (e) $2\frac{12}{8}$ (f) $4\frac{9}{4}$ (g) $1\frac{8}{12}$ (h) $3\frac{10}{5}$

22. Express each of the following as an improper fraction.

   (a) $1\frac{4}{7}$ (b) $2\frac{4}{5}$ (c) $3\frac{1}{8}$ (d) $2\frac{9}{10}$

23. Arrange the following numbers in increasing order.

   (a) $\frac{1}{3}, \frac{5}{6}, \frac{1}{12}$ (b) $1\frac{3}{4}, \frac{9}{4}, 1\frac{1}{4}$

   (c) $1\frac{3}{5}, \frac{9}{2}, 3$ (d) $2\frac{1}{5}, \frac{9}{4}, \frac{20}{6}$

24. What is the value of n in each of the following?

   (a) $2\frac{3}{8} = 1\frac{n}{8}$ (b) $3\frac{2}{7} = 2\frac{n}{7}$ (c) $4\frac{5}{6} = 3\frac{n}{6}$

25. Find the value of $9 \div 6$. Give the answer as a fraction in its simplest form.

26. Find the value of n in each of the following.

   (a) $5 \div 9 = \frac{n}{9}$ (b) $13 \div 5 = 2\frac{n}{5}$ (c) $10 \div 4 = 2\frac{n}{2}$

27. Juan painted $\frac{3}{10}$ of a pole red. The rest of the pole was **not** painted. What fraction of the pole was **not** painted?

28. Mary, Susan, and Ken shared a pizza. Mary and Susan each had $\frac{3}{8}$ of the pizza. What fraction of the pizza did Ken have?

29. Kenneth read $\frac{5}{12}$ of a novel on Monday. He read $\frac{1}{12}$ of it on Tuesday and $\frac{5}{12}$ of it on Wednesday. What fraction of the novel did he read altogether in the three days?

30. Gwen bought 1 liter of tomato juice. She drank $\frac{2}{7}$ of it in the morning. She drank $\frac{4}{7}$ of it in the evening. How much tomato juice was left?

31. Mrs. Williams bought 5 pizzas for a class party. There were 20 students in her class. How much of a pizza did each student get? Give your answer in its simplest form.

32. A rope 18 m long is cut into 4 equal pieces. What is the length of each piece in meters? Give your answer as a mixed number in its simplest form.

33. Shane was asked to express $\frac{14}{9}$ as a mixed number.

    (a) His answer was $1\frac{4}{9}$. Is he correct? Explain.

    (b) Show two different methods to express $\frac{14}{9}$ as a mixed number.

Review 3, pages 107–111

1 Adding and Subtracting Related Fractions

Chrissy, Sharon and Paul shared a pizza.

Chrissy ate $\frac{3}{8}$ of the pizza.

Sharon ate $\frac{1}{8}$ of the pizza.

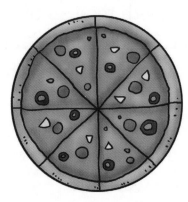

Paul ate $\frac{1}{4}$ of the pizza.

What fraction of the pizza did Chrissy and Sharon eat?

Add $\frac{3}{8}$ and $\frac{1}{8}$.

> The pizza is divided into 8 equal parts. Chrissy ate 3 parts and Sharon ate 1 part.
> 3 eighths + 1 eighth = 4 eighths

$$\frac{3}{8} + \frac{1}{8} = \frac{4}{8}$$

$$= \boxed{}$$

> Always write your answer in the simplest form.
> 4 eighths = 1 half

Chrissy and Sharon ate of the pizza.

What fraction of the pizza did they eat altogether?

$$\frac{3}{8} + \frac{1}{8} + \frac{1}{4} = \frac{3}{8} + \frac{1}{8} + \frac{2}{8}$$

$$= \boxed{}$$

$$= \boxed{}$$

One fourth of the pizza is the same as two eighths. Paul ate two eighths of the pizza.

We can also add $\frac{1}{2}$ and $\frac{1}{4}$.

$$\frac{1}{2} + \frac{1}{4} = \frac{\boxed{}}{4} + \frac{1}{4}$$

$$= \boxed{}$$

Before we add or subtract fractions, we change them to fractions with the same denominator.

Altogether, the three children

ate $\boxed{}$ of the pizza.

How much pizza was left?

$$1 - \frac{3}{4} = \frac{4}{4} - \frac{3}{4} = \frac{1}{4}$$

$$1 = \frac{4}{4}$$

1. (a) Add $\frac{3}{4}$ and $\frac{1}{8}$.

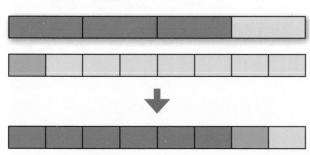

$$\frac{3}{4} + \frac{1}{8} = \frac{\boxed{}}{8} + \frac{1}{8}$$

$$= \frac{\boxed{}}{8}$$

Change $\frac{3}{4}$ and $\frac{1}{8}$ to like fractions first.

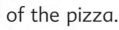

(b) Add $\frac{3}{4}$ and $\frac{5}{8}$.

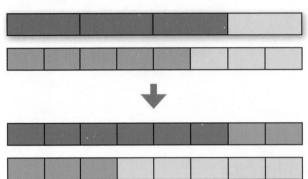

$$\frac{3}{4} + \frac{5}{8} = \frac{\boxed{}}{8} + \frac{5}{8}$$

$$= \frac{\boxed{}}{8}$$

$$= \boxed{}$$

When the result is an improper fraction, change it to a mixed number.

2. Add $\frac{4}{5}$ and $\frac{7}{10}$.

$$\frac{4}{5} + \frac{7}{10} = \frac{\boxed{}}{10} + \frac{7}{10}$$

$$= \frac{\boxed{}}{10}$$

$$= 1\frac{\boxed{}}{10}$$

$$= 1\frac{\boxed{}}{2}$$

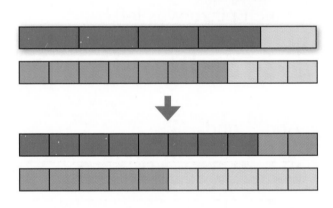

3. What are the missing numbers?

(a) $\dfrac{1}{2} + \dfrac{7}{8} = \dfrac{\boxed{}}{8} + \dfrac{7}{8}$

$= \dfrac{\boxed{}}{8}$

$= \dfrac{8}{8} + \dfrac{\boxed{}}{8}$

$= 1\dfrac{\boxed{}}{8}$

(b) $\dfrac{1}{3} + \dfrac{1}{6} = \dfrac{\boxed{}}{6} + \dfrac{1}{6}$

$= \dfrac{\boxed{}}{6}$

$= \dfrac{\boxed{}}{\boxed{}}$

(c) $\dfrac{7}{12} + \dfrac{2}{3} = \dfrac{7}{12} + \dfrac{\boxed{}}{12}$

$= \dfrac{\boxed{}}{12}$

$= 1\dfrac{\boxed{}}{\boxed{}}$

4. Add. Give each answer in its simplest form.

(a) $\dfrac{3}{5} + \dfrac{4}{5}$

(b) $\dfrac{7}{8} + \dfrac{5}{8}$

(c) $\dfrac{7}{12} + \dfrac{7}{12}$

(d) $\dfrac{1}{2} + \dfrac{1}{8}$

(e) $\dfrac{2}{5} + \dfrac{3}{10}$

(f) $\dfrac{3}{4} + \dfrac{1}{12}$

(g) $\dfrac{1}{2} + \dfrac{5}{6}$

(h) $\dfrac{5}{6} + \dfrac{7}{12}$

(i) $\dfrac{2}{3} + \dfrac{11}{12}$

(j) $\dfrac{1}{3} + \dfrac{1}{9} + \dfrac{2}{9}$

(k) $\dfrac{3}{4} + \dfrac{2}{8} + \dfrac{1}{8}$

(l) $\dfrac{3}{4} + \dfrac{1}{2} + \dfrac{5}{6}$

Exercise 1, pages 112–114

5. Subtract $\frac{1}{8}$ from $\frac{1}{2}$.

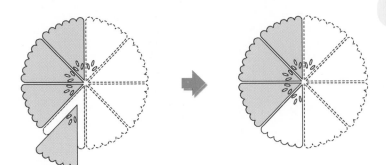

1 half = 4 eighths

$$\frac{1}{2} - \frac{1}{8} = \boxed{}$$

6. Subtract $\frac{1}{2}$ from $\frac{7}{8}$.

$\frac{1}{2} = \frac{\boxed{}}{8}$

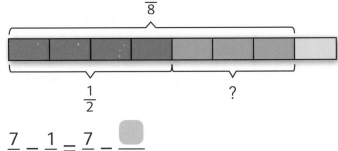

$\frac{7}{8}$

$\frac{1}{2}$?

$$\frac{7}{8} - \frac{1}{2} = \frac{7}{8} - \frac{\boxed{}}{8}$$

$$= \frac{\boxed{}}{8}$$

7. What are the missing numbers?

(a) $\frac{3}{4} - \frac{1}{8} = \frac{\boxed{}}{8} - \frac{1}{8}$

$= \frac{\boxed{}}{8}$

(b) $\frac{7}{10} - \frac{2}{5} = \frac{7}{10} - \frac{\boxed{}}{10}$

$= \frac{\boxed{}}{10}$

8. Subtract $\frac{5}{12}$ from $\frac{3}{4}$.

$\frac{3}{4} = \frac{\square}{12}$

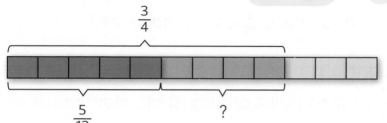

$\frac{3}{4}$

$\frac{5}{12}$?

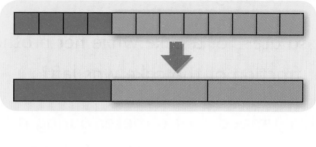

$\frac{3}{4} - \frac{5}{12} = \frac{\square}{12} - \frac{5}{12}$

$= \frac{\square}{12}$

$= \square$

9. What are the missing numbers?

(a) $\frac{7}{10} - \frac{1}{2} = \frac{7}{10} - \frac{\square}{10}$

$= \frac{\square}{10}$

$= \square$

(b) $\frac{2}{3} - \frac{5}{12} = \frac{\square}{12} - \frac{5}{12}$

$= \frac{\square}{12}$

$= \square$

10. Subtract.

(a) $\frac{5}{9} - \frac{1}{3}$

(b) $\frac{3}{4} - \frac{3}{8}$

(c) $\frac{4}{5} - \frac{7}{10}$

(d) $\frac{5}{6} - \frac{1}{2}$

(e) $\frac{1}{3} - \frac{1}{12}$

(f) $\frac{7}{10} - \frac{1}{5}$

(g) $\frac{1}{2} - \frac{1}{10}$

(h) $\frac{3}{4} - \frac{5}{12}$

(i) $\frac{5}{6} - \frac{7}{12}$

(j) $1 - \frac{1}{2} - \frac{1}{4}$

(k) $1 - \frac{1}{2} - \frac{1}{6}$

(l) $\frac{2}{3} - \frac{1}{6} - \frac{1}{3}$

Exercise 2, pages 115–116

11. Mary has $\frac{3}{4}$ of a liter of orange juice. She drinks $\frac{1}{2}$ of a liter of it. How much orange juice does she have left?

12. Mr. Johnson bought a can of paint. He used $\frac{1}{2}$ of it to paint a table. He used $\frac{1}{8}$ of it to paint a book shelf. How much paint did he use altogether?

13. Marissa ate $\frac{1}{3}$ of a cake while her brother ate $\frac{5}{12}$ of it. What fraction of the cake was left?

14. Marilyn jumped $\frac{5}{6}$ of a meter during a training session. Diana jumped $\frac{1}{3}$ of a meter further than Marilyn. How far did Diana jump?

15. Natalie spent $\frac{1}{5}$ of her allowance on some books and $\frac{7}{10}$ of it on a new backpack.
    (a) What fraction of her allowance did she spend?
    (b) What fraction did she have left?

16. Meredith bought $\frac{2}{5}$ of a kg of sugar. Courtney bought $\frac{1}{10}$ of a kg of sugar less than Meredith.

    (a) Find the mass of sugar bought by Courtney.
    (b) Find the total mass of sugar bought by both of them.

Exercise 3, pages 117–118

② Adding and Subtracting Mixed Numbers

(a) At a bakery, all the pies are the same size. Customers can buy whole pies, or slices. Each slice is $\frac{1}{6}$ of a pie. In the morning, $2\frac{5}{6}$ pies were sold. In the afternoon, $3\frac{4}{6}$ pies were sold. How many pies were sold that day?

$2\frac{5}{6} + 3\frac{4}{6}$

$2 + 3 = 5$

$\frac{5}{6} + \frac{4}{6} = \boxed{}$

$\phantom{\frac{5}{6} + \frac{4}{6}} = \boxed{}$

$5 + \boxed{} = \boxed{}$

$\boxed{}$ pies were sold.

(b) Find the total length of $3\frac{3}{4}$ m and $1\frac{5}{12}$ m.

$3\frac{3}{4}$m

$1\frac{5}{12}$ m

$3\frac{3}{4} + 1\frac{5}{12} = 4\frac{3}{4} + \frac{5}{12}$

$\phantom{3\frac{3}{4} + 1\frac{5}{12}} = 4\frac{9}{12} + \frac{5}{12}$

$\phantom{3\frac{3}{4} + 1\frac{5}{12}} = 4\frac{\boxed{}}{12} = \boxed{}$

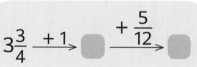

The total length is $\boxed{}$ m.

117

1. Add $4\frac{7}{12}$ and $1\frac{3}{4}$.

    $$4\frac{7}{12} + 1\frac{3}{4} = 5\frac{7}{12} + \frac{3}{4}$$

    $$= 5\frac{7}{12} + \frac{9}{12}$$

    $$= 5\frac{\boxed{}}{12}$$

    $$= 5\frac{\boxed{}}{3}$$

    $$= \boxed{}$$

2. Add.

    (a) $3\frac{7}{8} + 4\frac{3}{8} = 7\frac{7}{8} + \frac{3}{8}$

    $$= 7\frac{\boxed{}}{8}$$

    $$= \boxed{}$$

    (b) $2\frac{7}{12} + 1\frac{2}{3} = 3\frac{7}{12} + \frac{2}{3}$

    $$= 3\frac{7}{12} + \frac{\boxed{}}{12}$$

    $$= 3\frac{\boxed{}}{12}$$

    $$= \boxed{}$$

3. Add. Give each answer in its simplest form.

    (a) $6\frac{3}{5} + 2\frac{1}{5}$

    (b) $1\frac{5}{8} + 3\frac{3}{8}$

    (c) $5\frac{3}{10} + 1\frac{9}{10}$

    (d) $4\frac{2}{9} + 1\frac{4}{9}$

    (e) $1\frac{1}{6} + 1\frac{7}{12}$

    (f) $2\frac{7}{12} + 3\frac{3}{4}$

    (g) $4\frac{9}{10} + 2\frac{3}{10} + \frac{3}{10}$

    (h) $1\frac{5}{12} + 2\frac{3}{4} + 1\frac{3}{4}$

    (i) $2\frac{7}{10} + 3\frac{27}{100}$

Exercise 4, pages 119–120

4. Find the difference in length between $3\frac{3}{4}$ m and $1\frac{5}{12}$ m.

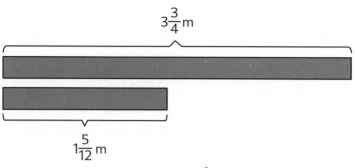

$3\frac{3}{4}$ m

$1\frac{5}{12}$ m

$$3\frac{3}{4} - 1\frac{5}{12} = 2\frac{3}{4} - \frac{5}{12}$$

$$= 2\frac{9}{12} - \frac{5}{12}$$

$$= 2\frac{\boxed{}}{12} = \boxed{}$$

$3\frac{3}{4} \xrightarrow{-1} \boxed{} \xrightarrow{-\frac{5}{12}} \boxed{}$

The difference in length is $\boxed{}$ m.

5. Subtract.

(a) $7\frac{1}{8} - 4\frac{3}{8} = 3\frac{1}{8} - \frac{3}{8}$

$$= 2\frac{\boxed{}}{8} - \frac{3}{8}$$

$$= 2\frac{\boxed{}}{8} = \boxed{}$$

(b) $3\frac{2}{5} - 1\frac{9}{10} = 2\frac{2}{5} - \frac{9}{10}$

$$= 2\frac{\boxed{}}{10} - \frac{9}{10}$$

$$= 1\frac{\boxed{}}{10} - \frac{9}{10}$$

$$= 1\frac{\boxed{}}{10} = \boxed{}$$

6. Subtract. Give each answer in its simplest form.

(a) $4\frac{7}{8} - 1\frac{3}{8}$

(b) $5\frac{1}{6} - 1\frac{5}{6}$

(c) $5\frac{3}{10} - 1\frac{9}{10}$

(d) $3\frac{1}{2} - 1\frac{3}{10}$

(e) $5\frac{1}{4} - 2\frac{7}{12}$

(f) $4\frac{7}{12} - 3\frac{3}{4}$

(g) $7 - 2\frac{3}{10} - \frac{7}{10}$

(h) $5\frac{5}{12} - \frac{2}{3} - 1\frac{2}{3}$

(i) $6\frac{7}{10} - 3\frac{27}{100}$

Exercise 5, pages 121–122

Add or subtract. Give each answer in its simplest form.

7. Ann jogged $2\frac{5}{8}$ miles on Saturday. She jogged $2\frac{7}{8}$ miles the next day.

   (a) On which day did she jog the longer distance? How much further did she jog?
   (b) How many miles did she jog altogether on both days?

8. There were $3\frac{1}{6}$ loaves of bread on the table. After breakfast, there were $1\frac{2}{3}$ loaves left. How many loaves of bread were eaten?

9. A container has a capacity of 3 liters. It contains $1\frac{3}{4}$ liters of water. How much more water is needed to fill the container completely?

10. Robert planned to spend $1\frac{1}{2}$ hours cooking a meal. He finished the cooking in $1\frac{1}{12}$ hours instead. How much earlier did he finish the cooking?

11. The total length of two ribbons is $2\frac{3}{4}$ m. If one ribbon is $1\frac{5}{8}$ m long, what is the length of the other ribbon?

12. Faith donated $1\frac{4}{5}$ kg of pet food to the animal shelter in January. She donated $2\frac{3}{10}$ kg of pet food in February. How many kilograms of pet food did she donate in the two months?

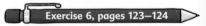

Exercise 6, pages 123–124

③ Multiplying a Fraction and a Whole Number

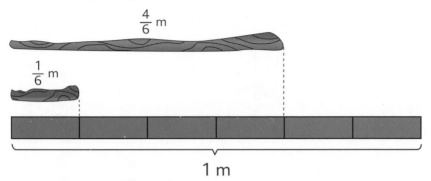

$\frac{4}{6}$ m

$\frac{1}{6}$ m

1 m

(a) $\frac{4}{6}$ m is ⬛ times as long as $\frac{1}{6}$ m.

$$\frac{1}{6} \times 4 = \frac{1}{6} + \frac{1}{6} + \frac{1}{6} + \frac{1}{6} = \frac{4}{6} = \frac{\blacksquare}{3}$$

(b) Sam drinks $\frac{1}{2}$ a liter of milk a day.
How many liters of milk will he drink in 5 days?

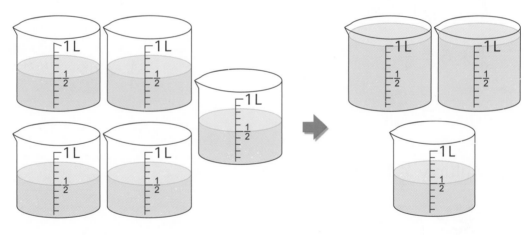

$\frac{1}{2} \times 5 = \frac{5}{2}$

$= 2\frac{1}{2}$

$\frac{1}{2} + \frac{1}{2} + \frac{1}{2} + \frac{1}{2} + \frac{1}{2} = \frac{5}{2}$

He will drink $2\frac{1}{2}$ liters of milk in 5 days.

$$\frac{1}{2} \times 5 = \frac{1 \times 5}{2}$$

1. Multiply $\frac{1}{2}$ by 8.

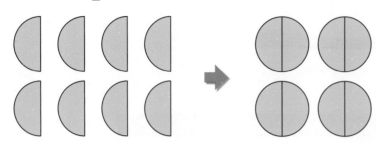

$\frac{1}{2} \times 8 = \frac{8}{2}$

$= $

$\boxed{\dfrac{1}{2} \times 8 = \dfrac{1 \times 8}{2}}$

2. Multiply $\frac{1}{4}$ by 6.

$\frac{1}{4} \times 6 = \frac{6}{4}$

$= $

$\boxed{\dfrac{1}{4} \times 6 = \dfrac{1 \times 6}{4}}$

3. Multiply $\frac{2}{3}$ by 4.

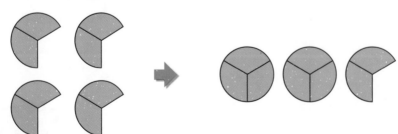

$\frac{2}{3} \times 4 = \frac{8}{3}$

$= $

$\boxed{\dfrac{2}{3} \times 4 = \dfrac{2 \times 4}{3}}$

4. Multiply. Give each answer in its simplest form.

(a) $\frac{1}{5} \times 3$ (b) $\frac{1}{3} \times 6$ (c) $\frac{1}{6} \times 8$

(d) $\frac{3}{8} \times 4$ (e) $\frac{7}{10} \times 5$ (f) $\frac{5}{12} \times 4$

Exercise 7, pages 125–126

5. Multiply 5 by $\frac{1}{2}$.

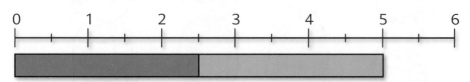

$5 \times \frac{1}{2} =$ ☐

$5 \times \frac{1}{2} = \frac{1}{2} \times 5$

6. Multiply 6 by $\frac{3}{4}$.

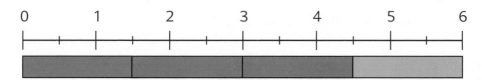

$6 \times \frac{3}{4} = \frac{18}{4}$

$= $ ☐

$6 \times \frac{3}{4} = \frac{6 \times 3}{4}$

7. Multiply. Give each answer in its simplest form.

(a) $2 \times \frac{1}{5}$ (b) $3 \times \frac{7}{8}$

(c) $3 \times \frac{2}{3}$ (d) $8 \times \frac{3}{4}$

(e) $9 \times \frac{1}{6}$ (f) $12 \times \frac{3}{8}$

Exercise 8, pages 127–128

4 Fraction of a Set

2 out of 5 children are girls.
What fraction of the children are girls?

2 out of 5 groups of children are girls.
What fraction of the children are girls?

2 out of 5 is $\frac{2}{5}$.

1. What fraction of each set is shaded?

(a)

(b)
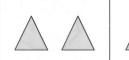

(c)
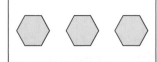

(d)
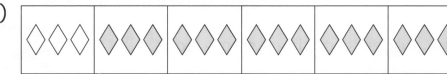

Exercise 9, pages 129–131

2. There are 8 coins.
   6 of them are dimes.
   What fraction of the coins are dimes?

   6 out of 8 is $\frac{6}{8}$.

   $\frac{6^3}{8_4} = \frac{3}{4}$

   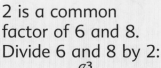
   2 is a common factor of 6 and 8. Divide 6 and 8 by 2:
   $\frac{6^3}{8_4}$

    of the coins are dimes.

3. Matthew had 42 pebbles. He lost 6 of them.
   What fraction of the pebbles did he lose?

   $\frac{6}{42} =$

   6 out of 42 is $\frac{6}{42}$.
   Express $\frac{6}{42}$ in its simplest form.

   He lost 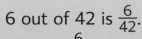 of the pebbles.

4. In a class of 40 students, 25 are boys. Express the number of girls as a fraction of the students in the class.

Method 1:

$40 - 25 = 15$

There are 15 girls.

$\frac{15}{40} = $

First, find the number of girls.

of the students in the class are girls.

Method 2:

$\frac{25}{40} = \frac{5}{8}$

First, express the number of boys as a fraction of the class.

$\frac{5}{8}$ of the students in the class are boys.

$1 - \frac{5}{8} = $

of the students in the class are girls.

Exercise 10, pages 132–134

5. What is $\frac{1}{3}$ of 12?

Divide 12 into 3 equal groups. One group is $\frac{1}{3}$ of 12. $\frac{1}{3}$ of 12 is 4.

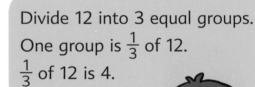

$\frac{1}{3}$ of 12 =

6. What is $\frac{3}{4}$ of 20?

$\frac{1}{4}$ of 20 =

$\frac{3}{4}$ of 20 =

Exercise 11, pages 135–136

7. Find the value of $\frac{3}{4}$ of 24.

$\frac{1}{4}$ of 24 $= \frac{24}{4}$

$= \boxed{}$

$\frac{1}{4}$ of 24 is the same as $\frac{24}{4}$.

$\frac{3}{4}$ of 24 $= 3 \times \frac{24}{4}$

$= 3 \times \boxed{}$

$= \boxed{}$

$\frac{3}{4}$ of 24 is the same as $3 \times \frac{24}{4}$.

8. Find the value of $\frac{5}{6}$ of 18.

$\frac{5}{6}$ of 18 $= 5 \times \frac{18}{6}$

$= 5 \times \boxed{}$

$= \boxed{}$

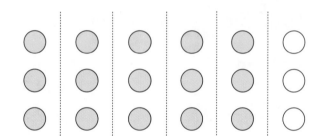

9. Find the value of $\frac{3}{8}$ of 120.

$\frac{1}{8}$ of 120 $= \frac{120}{8}$

$= \boxed{}$

$\frac{3}{8}$ of 120 $= \boxed{}$

10. Find the value of each of the following.

   (a) $\frac{1}{2}$ of 12

   (b) $\frac{1}{5}$ of 20

   (c) $\frac{1}{6}$ of 12

   (d) $\frac{2}{3}$ of 9

   (e) $\frac{3}{8}$ of 16

   (f) $\frac{2}{3}$ of 30

   (g) $\frac{1}{4}$ of 100

   (h) $\frac{3}{4}$ of 100

   (i) $\frac{3}{5}$ of 100

Exercise 12, pages 137–139

11. Kelley buys 24 flowers. $\frac{2}{3}$ of them are white.

How many white flowers are there?

Method 1:

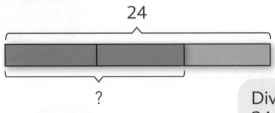

?

3 units = 24

1 unit =

2 units =

There are white flowers.

> Divide 24 into 3 equal parts.
> 24 = 3 units
> $\frac{2}{3}$ of 24 = 2 units

Method 2:

> $\frac{2}{3}$ of 24 is the same as $2 \times \frac{24}{3}$.

$\frac{2}{3} \times 24 = $

There are white flowers.

Exercise 13, pages 140–141

12. Alice had $20.

She used $\frac{2}{5}$ of it to buy a book.

How much did she have left?

Method 1:

$$\frac{2}{5} \times 20 = 2 \times \frac{20}{5}$$
$$= 8$$

She used $8.

> First, find the amount of money she used.

$20 - 8 = $

She had $ left.

Method 2:

$1 - \frac{2}{5} = \frac{3}{5}$

She had $\frac{3}{5}$ of her money left.

$\frac{3}{5} \times 20 = $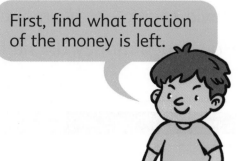

She had $\$$ ⬚ left.

First, find what fraction of the money is left.

Method 3:

$20

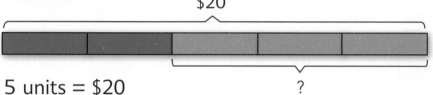

5 units = $20

1 unit = $ ⬚

3 units = $ ⬚

She had $\$$ ⬚ left.

?

Total	5 units
Used	2 units
Left	3 units

13. 48 children went to the zoo.

$\frac{3}{8}$ of them were girls.

How many boys were there?

$1 - \frac{3}{8} = \frac{5}{8}$

$\frac{5}{8}$ of the children were boys.

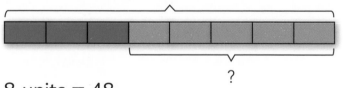

48

?

8 units = 48

1 unit = ⬚

5 units = ⬚

There were ⬚ boys.

Exercise 14, pages 142–144

14. David spent $\frac{2}{5}$ of his money on a book. The book cost $40. How much money did he have at first?

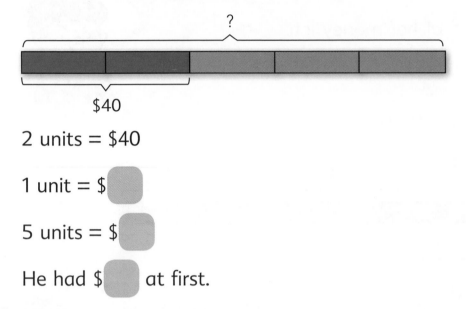

$40

2 units = $40

1 unit = $

5 units = $

He had $ at first.

15. Lily bought some picture cards. She gave $\frac{1}{3}$ of them to Matthew. If she gave 8 picture cards to Matthew, how many picture cards did she buy?

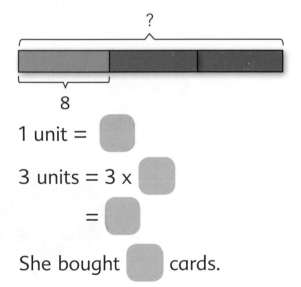

8

1 unit =

3 units = 3 x

=

She bought cards.

16. Victor buys $\frac{5}{8}$ kg of prawns each week. How many kilograms of prawns does he buy in 4 weeks?

17. Peter had a board 3 m long. He used $\frac{5}{12}$ of its length as a bookshelf. How long was the bookshelf?

18. Jane practices on the piano for $\frac{3}{4}$ of an hour a day. How many minutes does she practice each day?

19. In a class, $\frac{2}{5}$ of the students wear glasses.

    (a) What fraction of the students do **not** wear glasses?
    (b) If 16 students wear glasses, how many students are there altogether?

20. Nicole bought 30 eggs. She used $\frac{2}{3}$ of the eggs to bake cakes. How many eggs did she have left?

21. Kevin spent $\frac{3}{4}$ of his money on a book. If the book cost $24, how much money did he have at first?

22. Alan made 5 glasses of pineapple juice. If each glass contained $\frac{2}{5}$ liters of pineapple juice, how many liters of pineapple juice did Alan make altogether?

Exercise 15, pages 145–147

1. What fraction of the set are stars?

   (A) $\frac{1}{2}$ (B) $\frac{2}{5}$ (C) $\frac{3}{5}$ (D) $\frac{2}{3}$

2. What is the sum of $\frac{2}{5}$ and $\frac{7}{10}$?

   (A) $\frac{3}{10}$ (B) $\frac{9}{15}$ (C) $\frac{3}{5}$ (D) $1\frac{1}{10}$

3. What is the product of 4 and $\frac{2}{3}$?

   (A) $1\frac{1}{3}$ (B) $2\frac{2}{3}$ (C) $\frac{1}{3}$ (D) $4\frac{2}{3}$

4. Select True or False for the following.

   (a) $3 \times \frac{2}{9} < \frac{1}{9} \times 6$ True / False

   (b) $\frac{2}{3} \times 12 = \frac{2 \times 12}{3}$ True / False

5. Select True or False for the following.

   (a) $\frac{5}{8} + \frac{1}{4} = \frac{6}{12}$ True / False

   (b) $2\frac{1}{12} - 1\frac{5}{6} = \frac{1}{4}$ True / False

6. Write >, <, or = in place of each ⬤.

   (a) $\frac{7}{8} \times 2$ ⬤ $2\frac{7}{8}$

   (b) $\frac{2}{3} \times 5$ ⬤ $\frac{5}{3} + \frac{5}{3}$

7. Find the sum of each of the following. Give each answer in its simplest form.

   (a) $\frac{1}{3}$ and $\frac{5}{9}$

   (b) $\frac{2}{3}$ and $\frac{9}{12}$

   (c) $4\frac{5}{6}$ and $2\frac{1}{2}$

   (d) $3\frac{4}{5}$ and $7\frac{7}{10}$

   (e) $5\frac{7}{8}$ and $4\frac{3}{4}$

   (f) $6\frac{1}{6}$ and $3\frac{11}{12}$

8. Find the difference between each of the following. Give each answer in its simplest form.

   (a) $\frac{3}{4}$ and $\frac{7}{8}$

   (b) $\frac{11}{12}$ and $\frac{1}{3}$

   (c) 3 and $\frac{3}{7}$

   (d) $6\frac{1}{8}$ and $1\frac{1}{2}$

   (e) $3\frac{2}{5}$ and $\frac{1}{10}$

   (f) 4 and $1\frac{5}{8}$

Add or subtract. Give each answer in its simplest form.

	(a)	(b)	(c)
9.	$\frac{1}{4} + \frac{3}{8} + \frac{3}{4}$	$\frac{7}{12} + \frac{1}{4} + \frac{2}{3}$	$\frac{1}{2} + 1\frac{5}{6} + \frac{1}{12}$
10.	$\frac{9}{10} - \frac{1}{2} - \frac{1}{5}$	$1 - \frac{1}{4} - \frac{5}{12}$	$3\frac{8}{9} - \frac{2}{3} - 1\frac{2}{3}$

11. Find the value of each of the following. Give each answer in its simplest form.

(a) $15 \times \frac{1}{3}$ (b) $12 \times \frac{3}{4}$ (c) $40 \times \frac{9}{8}$

(d) $\frac{1}{4}$ of 28   (e) $\frac{5}{6}$ of 42   (f) $\frac{3}{4}$ of 200

(g) $\frac{5}{9}$ of $72   (h) $\frac{2}{3}$ of 27 kg   (i) $\frac{1}{5}$ of 350 m

12. Find the value of n in each of the following.

(a) $\frac{5}{8} + \frac{n}{16} = 1$ (b) $3\frac{5}{8} = 2 + n$ (c) $n \times \frac{1}{6} = \frac{5}{3}$

13. What fraction of each set is shaded?
Give each answer in its simplest form.

(a)

(b)

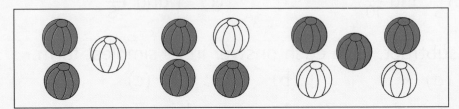

14. Gavin made a pie. He gave $\frac{3}{8}$ to his sister and $\frac{1}{4}$ to his neighbors. How much more pie did he give to his sister than to his neighbors?

15. Seth used $4\frac{2}{5}$ yd of rope to pitch a tent. Roger used $\frac{3}{10}$ yd less rope to pitch another tent. How many yards of rope did they use altogether?

16. Mr. Farell traveled $\frac{1}{3}$ of a trip on the first day. He traveled $\frac{4}{9}$ of the trip on the second day. He completed the trip on the third day. What fraction of the trip did he travel on the third day?

17. Maurice bought $2\frac{1}{8}$ kg of chicken wings and $1\frac{1}{4}$ kg of chicken thighs. He cooked $1\frac{3}{4}$ kg of the chicken wings and served them for dinner. How many kilograms of chicken did he have left?

18. 100 people attended a concert. 65 of them were women. Express the number of men as a fraction of the total number of people who attended the concert.

19.

Lily bought these items at half of the given prices. How much did she spend altogether?

20. Rebecca bought 600 g of potatoes. She used $\frac{3}{5}$ of the potatoes. How many grams of potatoes did she use?

21. A bucket of water can hold $\frac{4}{5}$ gal of water. The bucket was filled and emptied into a tank 8 times. How much water is in the tank?

22. Sarah had \$40. She used $\frac{3}{10}$ of it to buy a book. Find the cost of the book.

23. Mary cut a pizza into 16 slices. If she gave $\frac{3}{8}$ of the pizza to her friend, how many slices of pizza did she give away?

24. Mrs. Kelly has 56 pots of plants. 8 of them have flowers. What fraction of her potted plants have flowers?

25. There were 120 people at a concert. $\frac{2}{3}$ of them were adults. How many children were there?

26. Loraine bought a bottle of olive oil. She used $\frac{3}{10}$ of the oil. If she used 150 g of oil, how much oil did she buy?

27. Jordan poured 20 liters of water into an empty fish tank. If $\frac{5}{6}$ of the fish tank was filled, find the capacity of the tank.

28. $\frac{4}{5}$ of the children in a choir are girls.

    (a) What fraction of the children are boys?

    (b) If there are 8 boys, how many children are there in the choir?

    (c) How many more girls than boys are there in the choir?

29. After spending $\frac{3}{5}$ of her money on a tennis racket, Allison had $14 left. How much did the tennis racket cost?

30. Pauline bought a length of ribbon. She used $\frac{2}{5}$ of it to wrap a package and $\frac{1}{5}$ of it for a bow. If she used 60 in. of the ribbon, what was the length of the ribbon she bought?

31. Tom aims to run 5 rounds around a park within $1\frac{1}{2}$ hours. He takes $\frac{1}{3}$ of an hour to run 1 round. If he takes the same amount of time to run each round, will he succeed? Explain.

Review 4, pages 148–154

5 MEASURES

1 Looking Back

A sofa is about 6 feet and 9 inches long. How long is it in inches?

There are 12 inches in 1 foot.

Complete the table.

Feet	1	2	3	4	5	6	7	8	9	10
Inches	12									

1 ft = ⬜ in.

6 ft = ⬜ in.

6 ft 9 in. = ⬜ in. + 9 in.

= ⬜ in.

To change feet to inches, we multiply by 12.
1 ft = 1 × 12 = 12 in.
2 ft = 2 × 12 = 24 in.
...
6 ft = 6 × 12 = 72 in.

A coffee table is 36 inches long. How long is it in feet?

36 in. = ⬜ ft

To change inches to feet, we divide by 12.

138

Conversion of Measurements

Length
1 m = 100 cm
1 km = 1,000 m

1 yd = 3 ft
1 ft = 12 in.

Mass and Weight
1 kg = 1,000 g

1 lb = 16 oz

Capacity
1 L   = 1,000 ml

1 gal = 4 qt
1 qt = 2 pt
1 pt = 2 c

Time
1 year   = 12 months
1 week   = 7 days
1 day   = 24 hours
1 hour   = 60 minutes
1 minute = 60 seconds

1. Write 10 m in centimeters.

10 m = 10 × 100 = ☐ cm

2. The sofa is about 2 meters and 6 centimeters long.
How long is it in centimeters?

1 m = ☐ cm

2 m = ☐ × 100 = ☐ cm

2 m 6 cm = ☐ cm + 6 cm = ☐ cm

3. Write 500 cm in meters.

500 cm = ☐ m

cm	100	200	300	400	500
m	1	2	3	4	5

4. Write 325 cm in meters and centimeters.

325 cm = 300 cm + 25 cm = ☐ m + ☐ cm

5. A ribbon is 11 yd 2 ft.
   Write the length in feet.

   11 yd 2 ft = ☐ ft + 2 ft

   = ☐ ft

   To change yards to feet, we multiply by 3.

   1 yd = 1 × 3 = 3 ft
   2 yd = 2 × 3 = 6 ft

6. A sack of potatoes weighs 5 lb 10 oz.
   Write the weight in ounces.

   5 lb 10 oz = ☐ oz + 10 oz

   = ☐ oz

   1 lb = 1 × 16 = 16 oz
   5 lb = 5 × 16 = 80 oz

7. (a) Write 7 lb in ounces.

   7 lb = ☐ oz

oz	16	32	48	64	80	96	112
lb	1	2	3	4	5	6	7

   (b) Write 48 oz in pounds.

   48 oz = ☐ lb

8. (a) Write 8 yd in feet.

   8 yd = ☐ ft

   (b) Write 18 ft in yards.

   18 ft = ☐ yd

   To change feet to yards, we divide by 3.

   3 ft = 3 ÷ 3 = 1 yd
   6 ft = 6 ÷ 3 = 2 yd

9. Write in yards and feet.

   (a) 20 ft = ☐ yd ☐ ft

   20 ft
   ╱ ╲
   18 ft   2 ft

   (b) 25 ft = ☐ yd ☐ ft

   25 ÷ 3 = 8 R 1
   25 ft = 8 yd 1 ft

   (c) 422 ft = ☐ yd ☐ ft

   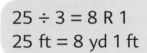

   3) 4 2 2

10. Find the missing numbers.

(a) 9 m = ☐ cm

(b) 8 days = ☐ hours

(c) 12 lb = ☐ oz

(d) 6 kg = ☐ g

(e) 4 yd = ☐ ft = ☐ in.

(f) 2 h = ☐ min = ☐ s

(g) 5 km = ☐ m = ☐ cm

(h) 3 gal = ☐ qt = ☐ pt

11. Find the missing numbers.

4 L = 4,000 ml
4,000 ml + 250 ml = ☐

(a) 4 L 250 ml = ☐ ml

(b) 5 km 40 m = ☐ m

(c) 4 years 5 months = ☐ months

(d) 1 hour 20 minutes = ☐ minutes

(e) 5 m 40 cm = ☐ cm

(f) 6 days 4 hours = ☐ hours

12. Find the missing numbers.

(a) 8 ft = ⬜ yd ⬜ ft

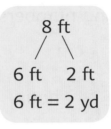

8 ft
6 ft   2 ft
6 ft = 2 yd

(b) 602 cm = ⬜ m ⬜ cm

(c) 2,400 g = ⬜ kg ⬜ g

(d) 30 days = ⬜ weeks ⬜ days

(e) 350 qt = ⬜ gal ⬜ qt

Exercise 1, pages 155–156

13. Subtract.

(a) 1 kg − 550 g

(b) 1 ft − 7 in.

(c) 1 h − 20 min

(d) 1 lb − 11 oz

14.  3 kg 450 g
7 lb 10 oz

 2 kg 650 g
5 lb 14 oz

(a) What is the total mass of both packages in kilograms and grams?

3 kg 450 g $\xrightarrow{\text{+ 2 kg}}$ 5 kg 450 g $\xrightarrow{\text{+ 650 g}}$ 6 kg 100 g

1,100 g = 1 kg 100 g

(b) What is the total weight of both packages in pounds and ounces?

$$7 \text{ lb } 10 \text{ oz} \xrightarrow{+ 5 \text{ lb}} 12 \text{ lb } 10 \text{ oz} \xrightarrow{+ 14 \text{ oz}} 13 \text{ lb } 8 \text{ oz}$$

> 24 oz = 1 lb 8 oz

(c) What is the difference in mass?

$$3 \text{ kg } 450 \text{ g} \xrightarrow{- 2 \text{ kg}} 1 \text{ kg } 450 \text{ g} \xrightarrow{- 650 \text{ g}} 800 \text{ g}$$

> 1 kg − 650 g = 350 g
> 350 g + 450 g = 800 g

(d) What is the difference in weight?

$$7 \text{ lb } 10 \text{ oz} \xrightarrow{- 5 \text{ lb}} 2 \text{ lb } 10 \text{ oz} \xrightarrow{- 14 \text{ oz}} 1 \text{ lb } 12 \text{ oz}$$

> 1 lb − 14 oz = 2 oz

15. Add or subtract in compound units.

(a) 20 ft 9 in. + 16 ft 10 in. = ⬚ ft ⬚ in.

(b) 40 kg 20 g − 5 kg 400 g = ⬚ kg ⬚ g

(c) 5 min 20 s + 6 min 40 s = ⬚ min ⬚ s

(d) 13 gal 1 qt − 4 gal 3 qt = ⬚ gal ⬚ qt

16. The total weight of two watermelons is 20 lb. The larger watermelon weighs 13 lb 9 oz. What is the weight of the smaller watermelon?

20 lb

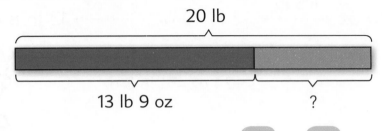

13 lb 9 oz   ?

The smaller watermelon weighs  lb ⬜ oz.

17. Three beakers contain 1 L 450 ml, 650 ml, and 1 L 20 ml of solution respectively. What is the total amount of solution in the three beakers?

The total amount of solution in the three beakers is

⬜ L ⬜ ml.

Exercise 2, pages 157–158

② Multiplying and Dividing Compound Measures

The 3 packages are of the same mass.
Each of them has a mass of 1 kg 200 g.
What is the total mass of the 3 packages?

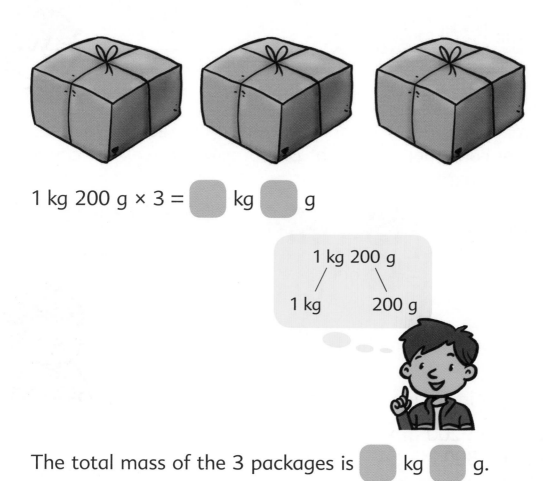

1 kg 200 g × 3 = ⬜ kg ⬜ g

1 kg 200 g
  ╱   ╲
1 kg   200 g

The total mass of the 3 packages is ⬜ kg ⬜ g.

1. The distance around a track was 1 km 300 m. Alex ran round the track 4 times. How far did he run?

1 km 300 m × 4 = ⬜ km ⬜ m

1 km 300 m
⟋   ⟍
1 km   300 m

He ran ⬜ km ⬜ m.

2. Gerald filled a tank completely with 4 buckets of water. Each bucket contained 2 gal 3 qt of water. What was the capacity of the tank?

2 gal 3 qt × 4 = ⬜ gal ⬜ qt

= ⬜ gal

2 gal 3 qt × 4
⟋   ⟍
2 gal   3 qt

The capacity of the bucket was ⬜ gal.

3. Multiply in compound units.

   (a) 3 km 200 m × 5
   (b) 4 L 300 ml × 4
   (c) 2 h 20 min × 5
   (d) 5 kg 200 g × 3
   (e) 6 m 20 cm × 6
   (f) 3 yd 2 ft × 7

Exercise 3, page 159

4. Jane cut a ribbon 5 m 20 cm long into 4 equal pieces to make flowers. What was the length of each piece?

5 m 20 cm ÷ 4 = ⬜ m ⬜ cm

5 m 20 cm
⟋   ⟍
4 m   120 cm

The length of each piece was ⬜ m ⬜ cm.

5. If the total mass of 5 bags of flour is 5 kg 650 g, find the mass of each bag of flour.

5 kg 650 g ÷ 5 = ⬜ kg ⬜ g

The mass of each bag of flour is ⬜ kg ⬜ g.

6. A tailor took 7 hours 30 minutes to sew 6 shirts. How long did he take to sew one shirt?

7 h 30 min = 6 h 90 min

7 h 30 min ÷ 6 = ☐ h ☐ min

He took ☐ h ☐ min to sew one shirt.

7. Marina poured 3 L 200 ml of milk equally into 8 glasses. How many milliliters of milk were there in each glass?

1 L = 1,000 ml
3 L 200 ml = ☐ ml

3 L 200 ml ÷ 8 = ☐ ml

There were ☐ ml of milk in each glass.

8. Divide in compound units.

(a) 2 L 240 ml ÷ 2
(b) 5 km 300 m ÷ 2
(c) 1 h 30 min ÷ 5
(d) 4 kg 500 g ÷ 3
(e) 2 m 60 cm ÷ 4
(f) 4 ft 3 in. ÷ 3

Exercise 4, page 160

148

9. Mrs. Gray used 2 bottles of syrup to make drinks. Each bottle contained 1 L 275 ml of syrup. How much syrup did she use?

10. Kent bought 3 kg 570 g of beans. He packed them equally into 3 bags. What was the mass of the beans in each bag?

11. Henry spent 3 hours 30 minutes every morning painting his house. He finished painting his whole house in 5 mornings. How much time did he spend painting his whole house?

12. A pineapple has a mass of 1 kg 800 g. A watermelon is 3 times as heavy as the pineapple.
    (a) What is the mass of the watermelon?
    (b) What is the total mass of the two fruits?

13. Maureen worked 8 hours 30 minutes every day. She was paid $8 each hour. How much did she earn in 6 days?

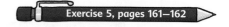

Exercise 5, pages 161–162

③ Measures and Fractions

(a) How many centimeters are in $\frac{3}{5}$ of a meter?

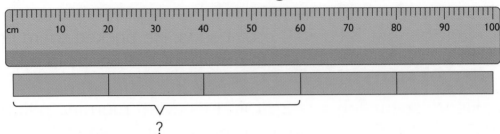

?

$$\frac{3}{5} \text{ m} = \frac{3}{5} \times 100 \text{ cm}$$

$$= \boxed{} \text{ cm}$$

1 m = 100 cm

(b) How many inches are in $1\frac{3}{4}$ feet?

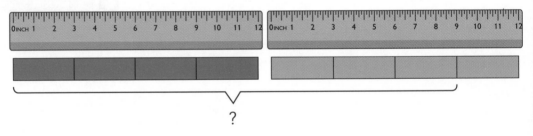

?

$$\frac{1}{4} \text{ of a foot} = \frac{1}{4} \text{ ft} = \frac{1}{4} \times 12 = 3 \text{ in.}$$

$$\frac{3}{4} \text{ ft} = 3 \times \boxed{} \text{ in.} = \boxed{} \text{ in.}$$

$$1\frac{3}{4} \text{ ft} = 12 \text{ in.} + \boxed{} \text{ in.} = \boxed{} \text{ in.}$$

1. An apple weighs $\frac{3}{8}$ of a pound. How many ounces does it weigh?

$\frac{3}{8}$ lb = $\frac{3}{8}$ × 16 = ⬜ oz

2. How many months are there in $\frac{5}{6}$ of a year?

1 year = 12 months

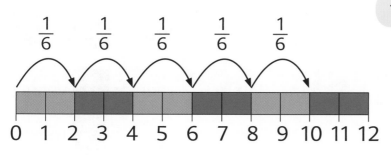

$\frac{5}{6}$ of a year = $\frac{5}{6}$ × 12 months

= ⬜ months

3. Find the missing numbers.

(a) $\frac{1}{2}$ min = ⬜ s

(b) $\frac{7}{10}$ kg = ⬜ g

(c) $\frac{2}{5}$ km = ⬜ m

(d) $\frac{3}{10}$ L = ⬜ ml

(e) $\frac{3}{4}$ year = ⬜ months

(f) $\frac{1}{6}$ h = ⬜ min

(g) $\frac{2}{3}$ yd = ⬜ ft

(h) $\frac{1}{4}$ lb = ⬜ oz

(i) $\frac{3}{4}$ gal = ⬜ qt

4. Express $2\frac{3}{4}$ h in hours and minutes.

$\frac{3}{4}$ h $= \frac{3}{4} \times 60$ min $=$ ◻ min

$2\frac{3}{4}$ h $=$ ◻ h ◻ min

5. Find the missing number in each ◻.

(a) $2\frac{1}{3}$ h $=$ ◻ h ◻ min   (b) $4\frac{2}{3}$ yd $=$ ◻ yd ◻ ft

(c) $5\frac{1}{4}$ gal $=$ ◻ gal ◻ qt   (d) $3\frac{1}{2}$ km $=$ ◻ km ◻ m

(e) $14\frac{9}{10}$ L $=$ ◻ L ◻ ml   (f) $6\frac{1}{4}$ years $=$ ◻ years

◻ months

Exercise 6, pages 163–164

6.  The total amount of water is $3\frac{3}{4}$ liters.

How many milliliters of water are there?

3 L $= 3,000$ ml

$\frac{3}{4}$ L $= \frac{3}{4} \times 1,000 =$ ◻ ml

$3\frac{3}{4}$ L $=$ ◻ ml

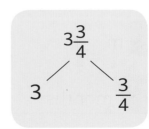

7. Express $3\frac{2}{5}$ km in meters.

3 km $= 3,000$ m

$3\frac{2}{5}$ km $= 3$ km $+ \frac{2}{5}$ km

$\frac{2}{5}$ km $= \frac{2}{5} \times 1,000$ m

$= \boxed{}$ m

$3\frac{2}{5}$ km $= \boxed{}$ m

8. Express $2\frac{1}{4}$ days in hours.

2 days $= \boxed{}$ h

$\frac{1}{4}$ day $= \boxed{}$ h

$2\frac{1}{4}$ days $= \boxed{}$ h

9. Find the missing numbers.

(a) $2\frac{1}{2}$ m $= \boxed{}$ cm

(b) $1\frac{1}{2}$ lb $= \boxed{}$ oz

(c) $3\frac{1}{2}$ gal $= \boxed{}$ qt

(d) $2\frac{3}{4}$ years $= \boxed{}$ months

(e) $1\frac{3}{10}$ L $= \boxed{}$ ml

(f) $4\frac{1}{3}$ min $= \boxed{}$ s

(g) $2\frac{1}{10}$ km $= \boxed{}$ m

(h) $3\frac{1}{3}$ h $= \boxed{}$ min

(i) $5\frac{3}{4}$ ft $= \boxed{}$ in.

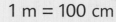

Exercise 7, pages 165–166

10. Jenny's handspan is 16 cm.
What fraction of 1 m is 16 cm?

$\dfrac{16}{100} = \boxed{}$

16 cm is $\boxed{}$ of 1 m.

1 m = 100 cm

11. What fraction of 1 day is 8 hours?

$$\frac{8}{24} = \boxed{}$$

8 h is $\boxed{}$ of a day.

12. Adam's stride is 75 cm. Express 75 cm as a fraction of 1 m.

75 cm

$$\frac{75}{100} = \boxed{}$$

75 cm is $\boxed{}$ of 1 m.

13. (a) What fraction of $2 is 80¢?

      $2 = 200¢ $1 = 100¢

$$\frac{80}{200} = \boxed{}$$

  (b) Express 600 ml as a fraction of 1 liter.
  (c) Express 90 cm as a fraction of 3 m.
  (d) Express 45 seconds as a fraction of 1 minute.
  (e) Express 50 minutes as a fraction of 2 hours.
  (f) Express 12 oz as a fraction of 1 lb.
  (g) Express 16 in. as a fraction of 4 ft.

Exercise 8, pages 167–168

1. Morris made 8 L 75 ml of fruit punch. How much fruit punch did he make in milliliters?

   (A) 8,750 ml   (B) 8,075 ml
   (C) 875 ml   (D) 87,500 ml

2. Ruth ran 2 km 950 m last week. Tricia ran 3 times as far. How much further did Tricia run than Ruth?

   (A) 5 km 900 m   (B) 5 km 950 m
   (C) 6 km 950 m   (D) 8 km 850 m

3. What fraction of 1 gal is 4 c?

   (A) $\frac{4}{1}$ (B) $\frac{1}{2}$ (C) $\frac{1}{4}$ (D) $\frac{1}{8}$

4. Select True or False for the following.

   (a) 3 h 15 min × 4 < 13 h   True / False
   (b) 6 m 20 cm ÷ 5 = 1 m 4 cm   True / False

5. Select True or False for the following.

   (a) $\frac{3}{4}$ of 2 ft > 9 in.   True / False

   (b) $1\frac{5}{12}$ years < 15 months   True / False

6. (a) Find the number of inches in 3 yards.
   (b) Find the number of centimeters in 4 kilometers.

7. Find the value of each of the following.

   (a) 2 km 740 m + 3 km 590 m   (b) 16 lb − 3 lb 10 oz
   (c) 1 h 25 min + 2 h 45 min   (d) 40 ft 5 in. − 6 ft 10 in.
   (e) 3 L 450 ml × 3   (f) 3 yd 2 ft × 12
   (g) 2 h 45 min × 3   (h) 3 h 20 min ÷ 2

Find the missing numbers.

| | (a) | (b) |

8. 8 lb = ☐ oz   120 L = ☐ ml

9. 26 months = ☐ years   37 in. = ☐ ft

10. $\frac{2}{3}$ h = ☐ min $\frac{2}{5}$ kg = ☐ g

11. $\frac{4}{5}$ m = ☐ cm $\frac{9}{10}$ km = ☐ m

12. $8\frac{3}{4}$ years = ☐ years $3\frac{3}{5}$ L = ☐ L ☐ ml

       = ☐ months

13. $9\frac{1}{4}$ lb = ☐ lb ☐ oz $5\frac{1}{3}$ h = ☐ h ☐ min

14. $3\frac{1}{2}$ ft = ☐ in. $4\frac{1}{4}$ gal = ☐ qt

15. $2\frac{7}{10}$ km = ☐ km ☐ m $4\frac{2}{3}$ days = ☐ days ☐ h

16. 1 day = ☐ h   6 gal = ☐ qt

         = ☐ min   = ☐ pt

                                        = ☐ c

17. Write >, <, or = in place of each ◯ .

(a) $4\frac{3}{4}$ ft ◯ 4 ft 8 in.

(b) 2 kg 70 g × 3 ◯ 6 kg 210 g

(c) 6 m 66 cm ÷ 6 ◯ 111 cm

(d) 1 L 5 ml × 4 ◯ 420 ml

18. (a) Express 50 minutes as a fraction of 2 hours.
    (b) Express 6 inches as a fraction of 4 feet.
    (c) Express 750 ml as a fraction of 3 L.
    (d) Express 80 cm as a fraction of 2 m.

19. A ribbon 32 yards long is cut into 8 equal pieces. How many feet is each piece?

20. A bucket can hold 6 gallons of water. If it is $\frac{3}{4}$ full, how many quarts of water does it contain?

21. Paul had 8 pieces of rope, each $4\frac{3}{4}$ m long.

    (a) What was the total length of the 8 pieces in meters?
    (b) What was the total length of the 8 pieces in centimeters?

22. The amount of information that can be stored by a computer is measured in bits. There are 8 bits in 1 byte and 1,024 bytes in 1 kilobyte.
    (a) How many bytes are there in 4 kilobytes?
    (b) How many bits are there in 1 kilobyte?
    (c) How many bytes are there in 1,024 bits?

23. A 5-oz carton of cherries at a farmer's market costs $1. Mary wants to buy cherries only if they are less than $3 a pound. Should she buy the cherries? Explain.

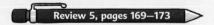 Review 5, pages 169–173

GLOSSARY

Word	Meaning
equivalent fractions	**Equivalent fractions** are fractions that are equal in value. $\frac{1}{3} = \frac{2}{6} = \frac{3}{9}$
expanded form	We write the **expanded form** of the number 23,546 like this: $20{,}000 + 3{,}000 + 500 + 40 + 6$
factors	$2 \times 3 \times 4 = 12$ 2, 3 and 4 are **factors** of 12.
improper fractions	An **improper fraction** is a fraction that is equal to or greater than 1. $\frac{3}{3}, \quad \frac{4}{3}, \quad \frac{5}{3}$
mixed number	When we add a whole number and a fraction, the result is a **mixed number**. $1\frac{1}{2}$ and $3\frac{3}{4}$ are **mixed numbers**.
multiples	The first 5 **multiples** of 3 are 3, 6, 9, 12 and 15.
standard form	70,639 is how we write the **standard form** of the number seventy thousand, six hundred, thirty-nine.

Grade 4 Curriculum Map

Common Core State Standards		Unit	Student Textbook Lessons	Student Workbook Exercises
OPERATIONS & ALGEBRAIC THINKING				
Use the four operations with whole numbers to solve problems.				
4.OA.1	Interpret a multiplication equation as a comparison, for example, interpret 35 = 5 × 7 as a statement that 35 is 5 times as many as 7 and 7 times as many as 5. Represent verbal statements of multiplicative comparisons as multiplication equations.	**Unit 2 Lesson 2 Multiplication by a 1-digit Number**	TB 4A: 51, 56–57	WB 4A: 52–54, 56–58
4.OA.2	Multiply or divide to solve word problems involving multiplicative comparison, for example, by using drawings and equations with a symbol for the unknown number to represent the problem, distinguishing multiplicative comparison from additive comparison.	**Unit 2 Lesson 3 Division by Ones and Tens**	TB 4A: 67–71	WB 4A: 64–65
4.OA.3	Solve multi-step word problems posed with whole numbers and having whole-number answers using the four operations, including problems in which remainders must be interpreted. Represent these problems using equations with a letter standing for the unknown quantity. Assess the reasonableness of answers using mental computation and estimation strategies including rounding.	**Unit 2 Lesson 2 Multiplication by a 1-digit Number** **Unit 2 Lesson 3 Division by Ones and Tens**	TB 4A: 56–57, 66–71	WB 4A: 56–58, 66–65
Gain familiarity with factors and multiples.				
4.OA.4	Find all factor pairs for a whole number in the range 1–100. Recognize that a whole number is a multiple of each of its factors. Determine whether a given whole number in the range 1–100 is a multiple of a given 1-digit number. Determine whether a given whole number in the range 1–100 is prime or composite.	**Unit 1 Lesson 3 Multiples** **Unit 1 Lesson 4 Factors**	TB 4A: 24–33	WB 4A: 21–22, 23–24, 25–28

159

Common Core State Standards		Unit	Student Textbook Lessons	Student Workbook Exercises
Generate and analyze patterns.				
4.OA.5	Generate a number or shape pattern that follows a given rule. Identify apparent features of the pattern that were not explicit in the rule itself. *For example, given the rule 'Add 3' and the starting number 1, generate terms in the resulting sequence and observe that the terms appear to alternate between odd and even numbers. Explain informally why the numbers will continue to alternate in this way.*	**Unit 1 Lesson 1 Numbers to 1,000,000**	**TB 4A:** 18–19	**WB 4A:** 14–15
NUMBER & OPERATIONS IN BASE TEN				
Generalize place-value understanding for multidigit whole numbers.				
4.NBT.1	Recognize that in a multidigit whole number, a digit in one place represents ten times what it represents in the place to its right. *For example, recognize that 700 ÷ 70 = 10 by applying concepts of place value and division.*	**Unit 1 Lesson 1 Numbers to 1,000,000**	**TB 4A:** 20	**WB 4A:** 16–18
4.NBT.2	Read and write multidigit whole numbers using base-ten numerals, number names, and expanded form. Compare two multidigit numbers based on meanings of the digits in each place, using >, =, and < symbols to record the results of comparisons.	**Unit 1 Lesson 1 Numbers to 1,000,000**	**TB 4A:** 8–17	**WB 4A:** 7–9, 10–12, 13
4.NBT.3	Use place-value understanding to round multidigit whole numbers to any place.	**Unit 1 Lesson 2 Approximation**	**TB 4A:** 21–23	**WB 4A:** 19–20
Use place-value understanding and properties of operations to perform multidigit arithmetic.				
4.NBT.4	Fluently add and subtract multidigit whole numbers using the standard algorithm.	**Unit 2 Lesson 1 Addition and Subtraction**	**TB 4A:** 42–50	**WB 4A:** 40–41, 42–43, 44–45, 46–47, 48–49, 50–51

Common Core State Standards		Unit	Student Textbook Lessons	Student Workbook Exercises
4.NBT.5	Multiply a whole number of up to four digits by a 1-digit whole number, and multiply two 2-digit numbers, using strategies based on place value and the properties of operations. Illustrate and explain the calculation by using equations, rectangular arrays, and/or area models.	**Unit 2 Lesson 2 Multiplication by a 1-digit Number** **Unit 2 Lesson 4 Multiplication by a 2-digit Number**	**TB 4A:** 51–56, 72–79	**WB 4A:** 52–54, 55, 66, 67, 68–70, 71–73
4.NBT.6	Find whole-number quotients and remainders with up to 4-digit dividends and 1-digit divisors, using strategies based on place value, the properties of operations, and/or the relationship between multiplication and division. Illustrate and explain the calculation by using equations, rectangular arrays, and/or area models.	**Unit 2 Lesson 3 Division by Ones and Tens**	**TB 4A:** 58–66	**WB 4A:** 59–60, 61–63
NUMBER & OPERATIONS — FRACTIONS				
Extend understanding of fraction equivalence and ordering.				
4.NF.1	Explain why a fraction $\frac{a}{b}$ is equivalent to a fraction $\frac{(n \times a)}{(n \times b)}$ by using visual fraction models, with attention to how the number and size of the parts differ even though the two fractions themselves are the same size. Use this principle to recognize and generate equivalent fractions.	**Unit 3 Lesson 1 Equivalent Fractions**	**TB 4A:** 84–88	**WB 4A:** 81–84, 85–86
4.NF.2	Compare two fractions with different numerators and different denominators, for example, by creating common denominators or numerators, or by comparing to a benchmark fraction such as $\frac{1}{2}$. Recognize that comparisons are valid only when the two fractions refer to the same whole. Record the results of comparisons with symbols >, =, or <, and justify the conclusions, for example, by using a visual fraction model.	**Unit 3 Lesson 1 Equivalent Fractions**	**TB 4A:** 86–88	**WB 4A:** 85–86

Common Core State Standards		Unit	Student Textbook Lessons	Student Workbook Exercises
Build fractions from unit fractions.				
4.NF.3	Understand a fraction $\frac{a}{b}$ with $a > 1$ as a sum of fractions $\frac{1}{b}$.	**Unit 3 Lesson 2 Adding and Subtracting Like Fractions**	**TB 4A:** 89	
4.NF.3a	Understand addition and subtraction of fractions as joining and separating parts referring to the same whole.	**Unit 3 Lesson 2 Adding and Subtracting Like Fractions**	**TB 4A:** 89–93	**WB 4A:** 87–90
4.NF.3b	Decompose a fraction into a sum of fractions with the same denominator in more than one way, recording each decomposition by an equation. Justify decompositions, for example, by using a visual fraction model. *Examples:* $\frac{3}{8} = \frac{1}{8} + \frac{1}{8} + \frac{1}{8}; \frac{3}{8} = \frac{1}{8} + \frac{2}{8};$ $2\frac{1}{8} = 1 + 1 + \frac{1}{8} = \frac{8}{8} + \frac{8}{8} + \frac{1}{8}.$	**Unit 3 Lesson 2 Adding and Subtracting Like Fractions**	**TB 4A:** 89	
4.NF.3c	Add and subtract mixed numbers with like denominators, for example, by replacing each mixed number with an equivalent fraction, and/or by using properties of operations and the relationship between addition and subtraction.	**Unit 4 Lesson 2 Adding and Subtracting Mixed Numbers**	**TB 4A:** 117–120	**TB 4A:** 119–120, 121–122, 123–124
4.NF.3d	Solve word problems involving addition and subtraction of fractions referring to the same whole and having like denominators, for example, by using visual fraction models and equations to represent the problem.	**Unit 3 Lesson 2 Adding and Subtracting Like Fractions**	**TB 4A:** 90–94	**WB 4A:** 87–90, 91–93

Common Core State Standards		Unit	Student Textbook Lessons	Student Workbook Exercises
4.NF.4	Apply and extend previous understandings of multiplication to multiply a fraction by a whole number.	**Unit 4 Lesson 3 Multiplying a Fraction and a Whole Number** **Unit 4 Lesson 4 Fraction of a Set**	**TB 4A:** 121–127	**WB 4A:** 127–128, 129–131, 135–136, 137–139
4.NF.4a	Understand a fraction $\frac{a}{b}$ as a multiple of $\frac{1}{b}$. *For example, use a visual fraction model to represent $\frac{5}{4}$ as the product $5 \times \left(\frac{1}{4}\right)$, recording the conclusion by the equation $\frac{5}{4} = 5 \times \left(\frac{1}{4}\right)$.*	**Unit 4 Lesson 3 Multiplying a Fraction and a Whole Number**	**TB 4A:** 121–122	
4.NF.4b	Understand a multiple of $\frac{a}{b}$ as a multiple of $\frac{1}{b}$, and use this understanding to multiply a fraction by a whole number. *For example, use a visual fraction model to express $3 \times \left(\frac{2}{5}\right)$ as $6 \times \left(\frac{1}{5}\right)$, recognizing this product as $\frac{6}{5}$. [In general, $n \times \left(\frac{a}{b}\right) = \frac{(n \times a)}{b}$.]*	**Unit 4 Lesson 3 Multiplying a Fraction and a Whole Number** **Unit 4 Lesson 4 Fraction of a Set**	**TB 4A:** 123–127	**WB 4A:** 127–128, 129–131, 135–136, 137–139
4.NF.4c	Solve word problems involving multiplication of a fraction by a whole number, for example, by using visual fraction models and equations to represent the problem. *For example, if each person at a party will eat $\frac{3}{8}$ of a pound of roast beef, and there will be 5 people at the party, how many pounds of roast beef will be needed? Between what two whole numbers does your answer lie?*	**Unit 4 Lesson 4 Fraction of a Set**	**TB 4A:** 128–131	**WB 4A:** 140–141, 142–144, 145–147

Common Core State Standards		Unit	Student Textbook Lessons	Student Workbook Exercises
Understand decimal notation for fractions, and compare decimal fractions.				
4.NF.5	Express a fraction with denominator 10 as an equivalent fraction with denominator 100, and use this technique to add two fractions with respective denominators 10 and 100. *For example, express $\frac{3}{10}$ as $\frac{30}{100}$, and add $\frac{3}{10} + \frac{4}{100} = \frac{34}{100}$.*	**Unit 6 Lesson 2 Hundredths**	**TB 4B:** 20	**WB 4B:** 25–26
4.NF.6	Use decimal notation for fractions with denominators 10 or 100. *For example, rewrite 0.62 as $\frac{62}{100}$; describe a length as 0.62 meters; locate 0.62 on a number line diagram.*	**Unit 6 Lesson 1 Tenths** **Unit 6 Lesson 2 Hundredths**	**TB 4B:** 10–14, 18–21	**WB 4B:** 7–12, 13–15, 16–18
4.NF.7	Compare two decimals to hundredths by reasoning about their size. Recognize that comparisons are valid only when the two decimals refer to the same whole. Record the results of comparisons with the symbols >, =, or <, and justify the conclusions, for example, by using a visual model.	**Unit 6 Lesson 1 Tenths** **Unit 6 Lesson 2 Hundredths**	**TB 4B:** 12–13, 22–23	**WB 4B:** 13–15, 29–31, 32–33
Measurement & Data				
Solve problems involving measurement and conversion of measurements.				
4.MD.1	Know relative sizes of measurement units within one system of units including km, m, cm; kg, g; lb, oz; l, ml; hr, min, sec. Within a single system of measurement, express measurements in a larger unit in terms of a smaller unit. Record measurement equivalents in a two-column table. *For example, know that 1 ft is 12 times as long as 1 in. Express the length of a 4 ft snake as 48 in. Generate a conversion table for feet and inches listing the number pairs (1, 12), (2, 24), (3, 36), ...*	**Unit 5 Lesson 1 Looking Back**	**TB 4A:** 138–144	**WB 4A:** 155–156, 157–158

Common Core State Standards		Unit	Student Textbook Lessons	Student Workbook Exercises
4.MD.2	Use the four operations to solve word problems involving distances, intervals of time, liquid volumes, masses of objects, and money, including problems involving simple fractions or decimals, and problems that require expressing measurements given in a larger unit in terms of a smaller unit. Represent measurement quantities using diagrams such as number line diagrams that feature a measurement scale.	**Unit 5** **Lesson 1** **Looking Back** **Unit 5** **Lesson 2** **Multiplying and Dividing Compound Measures** **Unit 5** **Lesson 3** **Measures and Fractions** **Unit 7** **Lesson 1** **Addition and Subtraction** **Unit 7** **Lesson 2** **Multiplication** **Unit 7** **Lesson 3** **Division**	**TB 4A:** 142–149, 153–154 **TB 4B:** 44–46, 53–55, 63–65	**WB 4A:** 155–156, 157–158, 159, 160, 161–162, **WB 4B:** 61–63, 69–71, 81–83
4.MD.3	Apply the area and perimeter formulas for rectangles in real-world and mathematical problems. *For example, find the width of a rectangular room given the area of the flooring and the length, by viewing the area formula as a multiplication equation with an unknown factor.*	**Unit 9** **Lesson 1** **Rectangles and Squares** **Unit 9** **Lesson 2** **Composite Figures**	**TB 4B:** 109–115, 116–119	**WB 4B:** 140–144, 145–147, 148–149, 150, 151–152
Represent and interpret data.				
4.MD.4	Make a line plot to display a data set of measurements in fractions of a unit $(\frac{1}{2}, \frac{1}{4}, \frac{1}{8})$. Solve problems involving addition and subtraction of fractions by using information presented in line plots. *For example, from a line plot find and interpret the difference in length between the longest and shortest specimens in an insect collection.*	**Unit 10** **Lesson 2** **Line Plots**	**TB 4B:** 131–132	**WB 4B:** 161–162

Common Core State Standards		Unit	Student Textbook Lessons	Student Workbook Exercises
Geometric measurement: understand concepts of angle and measure angles.				
4.MD.5	Recognize angles as geometric shapes that are formed wherever two rays share a common endpoint, and understand concepts of angle measurement.	**Unit 8 Lesson 1 Points, Lines, Line Segments, Rays, and Angles** **Unit 8 Lesson 3 Measuring Angles**	**TB 4B:** 73, 77–82	**WB 4B:** 90, 99–100, 101–105, 106–108, 109–112
4.MD.5a	An angle is measured with reference to a circle with its center at the common endpoint of the rays, by considering the fraction of the circular arc between the points where the two rays intersect the circle. An angle that turns through $\frac{1}{360}$ of a circle is called a 'one-degree angle', and can be used to measure angles.	**Unit 8 Lesson 3 Measuring Angles**	**TB 4B:** 77	
4.MD.5b	An angle that turns through n one-degree angles is said to have an angle measure of n degrees.	**Unit 8 Lesson 3 Measuring Angles**	**TB 4B:** 77–78	
4.MD.6	Measure angles in whole-number degrees using a protractor. Sketch angles of specified measure.	**Unit 8 Lesson 3 Measuring Angles**	**TB 4B:** 79–80	**WB 4B:** 99–100, 101–105, 106–108
4.MD.7	Recognize angle measure as additive. When an angle is decomposed into nonoverlapping parts, the angle measure of the whole is the sum of the angle measures of the parts. Solve addition and subtraction problems to find unknown angles on a diagram in real world and mathematical problems, for example, by using an equation with a symbol for the unknown angle measure.	**Unit 8 Lesson 3 Measuring Angles**	**TB 4B:** 80–82	**WB 4B:** 101–105, 106–108, 109–112

Common Core State Standards		Unit	Student Textbook Lessons	Student Workbook Exercises
GEOMETRY				
Draw and identify lines and angles, and classify shapes by properties of their lines and angles.				
4.G.1	Draw points, lines, line segments, rays, angles (right, acute, obtuse), and perpendicular and parallel lines. Identify these in two-dimensional figures.	**Unit 8 Lesson 3 Measuring Angles** **Unit 8 Lesson 4 Perpendicular Lines** **Unit 8 Lesson 5 Parallel Lines**	**TB 4B:** 80, 83–85, 86–88	**WB 4B:** 101–105, 106–108, 113–114, 115–116, 117–118, 119–120
4.G.2	Classify two-dimensional figures based on the presence or absence of parallel or perpendicular lines, or the presence or absence of angles of a specified size. Recognize right triangles as a category, and identify right triangles.	**Unit 8 Lesson 6 Quadrilaterals** **Unit 8 Lesson 7 Triangles**	**TB 4B:** 89–95	**WB 4B:** 121–122, 123–125
4.G.3	Recognize a line of symmetry for a two-dimensional figure as a line across the figure such that the figure can be folded along the line into matching parts. Identify line-symmetric figures and draw lines of symmetry.	**Unit 8 Lesson 9 Line Symmetry**	**TB 4B:** 96–101	**WB 4B:** 128–129, 130–131

Index